M000266600

THE MIGHTY HAVE FALLEN

THE INSIDE STORY OF THE FBI'S INVESTIGATION INTO POLITICAL CORRUPTION

DEREK BLUFORD

TABLE OF CONTENTS

Foreword   xi

Preface   xv

Introduction   xix

Chapter 1   I
The Story of Me

Chapter 2   13
Entrepreneur at Heart

Chapter 3   27
The FBI

Chapter 4   33
The Promise That Failed

Chapter 5   35
A Corrupt System

Chapter 6   41
A Chess Player

Chapter 7   45
Confidential Human Source

Chapter 8   52
Favors

Chapter 9   58
Los Angeles

Chapter 10   64
Corruption Everywhere

Chapter 11   67
Taking Down a Monster

Chapter 12   73
AmeriCorps

Chapter 13   77
Destroying the United Black Mayors Organization

Chapter 14   82
A Natural

Chapter 15   87
The Life of an FBI Source

Chapter 16   96
New Haven

Chapter 17   105
Corrupt PACs

Chapter 18   110
Tension Escalates

Chapter 19   118
Stockton

Chapter 20   123
Venture Capital

Chapter 21   127
The Presidential Election

Chapter 22   135
A Changing Relationship

Chapter 23   138
Grand Juries

Chapter 24   143
The Fight Against Corruption

Chapter 25   146
Is Your Local Government Corrupt?

Epilogue   151

Photo Album   155
Notes   317

The Mighty Have Fallen
The Inside Story of the FBI's Investigation into Political Corruption
Copyright © 2020 by Derek Bluford

Derek Bluford supports the right to free expression and the value of copyright. The purpose of copyright is to encourage writers and artists to produce the creative works that enrich our culture.

All rights reserved.

No part of this publication may be reproduced in whole or in part, or stored in a retrieval system, or transmitted in any form or by any means, electronic, mechanical, photocopying, recording, or otherwise, without written permission of the author.

If you would like permission to use material from the book (other than for review purposes), please contact info@derekbluford.com. Thank you for your support of the author's rights.

Derek Bluford
980 9th Street, 16th Floor
Sacramento, CA 95814
www.DerekBluford.com

First Edition: October 2020

Library of Congress Cataloging-in-Publication Data applied for.
ISBN: 978-1-7347637-6-8 (hardcover)
ISBN: 978-1-7347637-4-4 (e-book)
ISBN: 978-1-7347637-3-7 (paperback)
ISBN: 978-1-7347637-5-1 (audio-book)

This book is dedicated to my family and the few honest politicians of America. In the court of law, they have always said the punishment should entail paying back "the people." It was my honor to serve not just my community, but our nation, by shining the spotlight on corruption from all sides.

A special thanks to David Beasley and former Mayor Marni Sawicki for helping me put this together.

It has been said:

In politics, nothing happens by accident.
If it happens, you can bet it was planned that way.

"As I reflect back on the last 8 years, I have to say that it has been my sincere honor and privilege to serve as your Mayor. And it is my hope that at the end of my final day, after two terms in office, that the people of this great city might look back at my tenure and believe that I left the city just a little bit better off."

— MAYOR KEVIN JOHNSON, DECEMBER 13, 2016

"Kevin Johnson leaves a legacy of accomplishment, scandal."

— *SACRAMENTO BEE,* DECEMBER 4, 2016

"You remember K.J., Sacramento. He slunk out of office and out of the spotlight three years ago, amid resurgent allegations that he molested girls. You already knew these stories when you elected the former NBA great to be your mayor—twice. Johnson's questionable behavior around young women became such an open secret that City Hall publicly reminded its elected officials to stop giving unsolicited hugs in 2013.

And yet Sacramento remained K.J.'s city, seemingly turning a blind eye to Johnson's underage accusers so that it could bask in the shadow of its celebrity mayor. Until the national media told the rest of the country what you already knew, and a national audience recoiled.

But now he's back."

— *SACRAMENTO NEWS & REVIEW,* NOVEMBER 14, 2019

FOREWORD

I used to believe in luck, or being in the right place at the right time, as a means of explaining some of the extraordinary opportunities I've experienced throughout my life. Not until 2013 did I know for sure there are no random chance meetings. There is no way to account, other than fate, for the fact that a 43-year-old single mother of two, a renter, a registered Democrat with no previous political experience in a highly red area of Florida, could beat out five men including the incumbent (all but one Republican) to become the first woman mayor of Cape Coral, Florida. Except that's exactly what I accomplished. As the eighth largest city in Florida, over 197,000 residents called the city home at the time of my election. With an MBA, I worked in the field of insurance for 25+ years with my most recent role that of VP of marketing. The same year I ran for mayor, I started my consulting business specializing in a marketing strategy. Having served four years as an elected official with a municipal budget of over $600 million, I know a few things about how local government works. From lobbying our federal and state officials to testifying in front of a Senate committee, as mayor, I had access to some of the most powerful people in the nation. So, when Derek's proposal to review his book on crime and politics came across my computer screen on a popular freelancer website, I just knew I had to reach out to him. Call our meeting fate or something else, I just knew I was supposed to know him. I credit the universe for bringing us together.

Throughout my term I would, along with my council, approve contracts, oversee the city manager, city attorney, and auditor's daily functions. With over 1,500 city employees, there were always projects to dig into and many opportunities to make a difference in how the city spent taxpayers' monies. As a representative government, voters expect the people they elect into office to work hard to uphold their ideals, but most importantly, they expect them to be honest. Given my background in insurance, my expertise was in processes and procedures, so I was naturally inquisitive whenever the "playing field" between the city and vendors seemed too inconsistent. I had heard third hand accounts about envelopes of money being handed to county commissioners prior to votes; however, I wouldn't come across anything truly egregious until the city audited our municipal owned charter school system's internal cash fund. The audit uncovered several key findings that needed to be reported to the state; however, the biggest take away was our $1.3 million internal cash fund had no policies and procedures set up to protect it from misuse or fraud. In fact, the audit highlighted hundreds of thousands of dollars missing without receipts or backup material justifying purchases. Once discovered, the players involved, from the superintendent to a principal to members of their own governing board, would do their best to cover up the wrongdoings. The situation would become so chaotic it would take a police investigation to finally lay out the truth. When the smoke cleared, both the superintendent and principal quit before criminal action could be taken against them, and the city manager, who disliked any kind of bad publicity, decided not to pursue getting the money back. All of this happened with what seemed as proper "oversight" from the public and city staff.

Derek literally stepped into one of those holes and is able to give readers an up close and personal account of his interactions with politicians and city staff as they make back door deals to secure city contracts worth millions of dollars in taxpayer monies virtually unchecked. He paints an honest picture of the corruption he personally witnessed happening all across the nation in big and small cities while working with the FBI as a confidential human source. Most important, the lessons of Derek's personal journey apply to all of us. His transparency on how he came to work with the FBI showcases how redemption can be good for the soul. Derek's motives for wanting to tell this story are clear—to shine a light on what can happen in politics when no one is paying attention. For you, the taxpayer, these "deals" take away millions of dollars that should go directly back into your community to add amenities like more police officers or fire personnel, or to build public spaces for all to enjoy. The corruption outlined in Derek's book affects everyone in your community—and for the small business owner, competing for these contracts can cost them everything.

After reading *The Mighty Have Fallen*, you will hopefully be inspired to start getting more involved in your own city's local politics. Without proper oversight by municipal and county boards made up of volunteers from the community like you, the kind of corruption Derek showcases over and over in this book will continue to go on unchecked. After reading his account, listening to the tapes, and viewing the photos and texts, my hope is that you will feel compelled to get involved to make sure this isn't happening in your own city. Volunteer for oversight boards, and if your city doesn't have many, demand them to be established. You can make a difference!

The Honorable Mayor Marni Sawicki
Cape Coral, Florida, first woman mayor (2013–2017)
Board of Director for the Florida League of Mayors and
US Conference of Mayors

PREFACE

My name is Derek Bluford. I am a confidential human source for the Federal Bureau of Investigation (FBI). My code name with the Bureau is "The Lobbyist" and I often work cases under an alias. The pathway leading up to this role is not what one would expect. Although when I was a child, I wanted to work in law enforcement and did briefly, some of my early life choices both prevented and made me pivot from that becoming a reality. I ended up going to college to earn a degree in legal studies and later pursed another degree for business.

My career was that of an entrepreneur. I have started and sold several companies. However, during the course of running one of my last companies, I broke the law. This is what ultimately led to my federal indictment in 2018 and an immediate meeting with the US Attorney's Office, the FBI, and my attorney.

There was no way of knowing what was ahead of me. The financial crime that I committed generally would had been prosecuted by the state of California. However, there were some elements that crossed over into federal law that opened the door for the US Attorney's Office to pursue the matter. Make no mistake, the government officials were not interested in me. In fact, the statute of limitation was almost over.

What the US Attorney's Office really wanted was access to a business associate of mine: the former NBA superstar and mayor of Sacramento, Kevin Johnson. I met Kevin at a restaurant in Sacramento, California, a few years prior and the two of us hit it off immediately. With my passion for starting technology companies and Kevin's interest in investing along with his network of politicians, CEOs, celebrities, and investors, going into business together was a no-brainer. The US Attorney's Office was pursuing me, ultimately to get to Mayor Kevin Johnson. It seemed that no matter where Kevin went, whether it be politics, education, or business, claims of sexual misconduct would always surface. Shortly before running for mayor, his wife and he opened a new charter school for underprivileged children in the Sacramento area. Once he was elected, he would go on to become the President of the US Conference of Mayors, which was a very prestigious position to hold. Having been a poker player, I always knew when to hold and when to fold. When the government showed its hand, I knew it was time to fold.

While the initial agreement was to help with the sole investigation into former Mayor Kevin Johnson, my work would later expand and I would end up assisting with other political corruption cases including several actively serving mayors, members of Congress, and presidential candidates. Some of the cases I have worked led to indictments of elected officials. Other indictments are just around the corner. However, during the Grand Jury proceedings of the Kevin Johnson investigation, the coronavirus caused a worldwide pandemic. For the most part, life was put on hold.

Throughout this perilous journey, I kept notes, took photos, and collected my own copies of the evidence that I was capturing to protect myself. After all, this was the government I was working for. I knew I was in the position I was in because what I had done was wrong, however, I did not want to find myself in another position by acting at the direction of the FBI. Having grown up in a world far from where I had ended up, I understood the importance of having "proof" in regard to legal matters and for others to believe you. My early years were formed by an abusive mother who was in law enforcement, and many times had violated my family's trust and my trust. Losing my way, like so many others who go from not having much to enjoying the glamorous life, I wanted to fit in. I wanted to BE that person everyone could look up to and be proud of. Ultimately, I have learned I do not need to have "things" to make others proud. Pride comes from within. Interacting with Kevin after he became mayor and being swept up in his world of manipulation, fraud, and favors, I cannot unsee the things I have seen. Corruption is at every level of our political system —from developers, government contractors, and elected officials to investors and residents who sit on various government boards and committees. Unfortunately, it's even in the FBI—unfairly targeting certain political parties while funding others. Throughout this experience, I encountered a lot of crazy events, and I believe the world needs to know about what could be happening at their very own city hall. These officials are people who are elected to do good for our cities and country, but somehow lose their way. They are taking advantage of the people who voted them into office and creating a hierarchy of influential people in their communities to continue reaping the benefits. Encouraging the everyday American to wake up to what is going on around them is what will prevent the situations I will outline in this book from continuing to happen. I am here to tell that story.

Although I am no professional author, I have done my best to keep this book in chronological order; however, I believe it would be helpful to know that at one point, I began actively working on several investigations at the same time with different offices.

INTRODUCTION

The story that follows is about greed, corruption, and what happens when no one is paying attention. The circumstances around these crimes involve mayors, members of Congress, presidential candidates, members of their staff, everyday constituents who sit on various governmental boards and committees . . . and me—Derek Bluford, a confidential human source for the Federal Bureau of Investigation (FBI). I was often referred to by my code name, "The Lobbyist." I worked several political corruption cases and often under an alias.

What I am offering is a glimpse into how the game of money and power is played in American politics. I will forewarn you—it is disturbing. I have been immersed in this world for so long, I am no longer surprised by what I see. I believe the stories I will outline in this book will be shocking to you, the reader, who most likely is not yet as jaded and cynical regarding what truly happens in our political system as I have become. This is a tale of crooked multimillion-dollar contracts, envelopes stuffed with cash, members of staff who will stop at nothing to make sure they remain loyal to their candidate, and developers, companies, lobbyists, and politicians who brazenly enrich themselves and those around them at the public's expense.

While the initial investigation revolves around Kevin Johnson, a former NBA star who became mayor of Sacramento, California, the crimes broaden as the FBI follows the path of dirty money and promises to Kevin's deep network of connections. Kevin was a man of great political potential and promise. He was president of the US Conference of Mayors, a leadership position that made him a national policy leader and gave him opportunities to grow his network further and wider than anyone realized—until now. With access to the White House, the upper echelons of the Senate and Congress, and influential community leaders such as Al Sharpton, Jesse Jackson, Barry Bonds, Hillary Clinton, Donald Stern, Magic Johnson, owners and players from the Sacramento Kings, Meg Whitman, and many others, his position would embolden him to believe he was untouchable. He seemed to have it all and be on top of his game, even with the sexual misconduct allegations surrounding him. Kevin married Michelle Rhee, a former school superintendent in Washington, DC, who was herself an educational reformer with great potential, once considered for the job of US Secretary of Education. They were America's model power couple: an African-American mayor of a large American city and the Asian-American education pioneer with a plan for improving inner-city schools. Their positions could have led to massive changes for good in how our nation's policies were formulated and who those policies benefited. With their elite network, their legacy could have been one of reform to benefit the impoverished, our judicial and school systems, and the underserved minority communities throughout the United States. However, power and greed would replace whatever ambition initially intended.

Kevin and Michelle were not just talking educational theory. Together, they had started a charter school in Sacramento, implementing the ideals they once envisioned. Just by looking at the couple, it was not hard to envision a more diverse, fair America in the making. With their charter school up and running, receiving large grants from various organizations, everything seemed to be finally reaching that point where their potential was turning into reality.

However, instead of continuing to pursue their dream of a fair and just America, Kevin chose money and greed over all else.

Kevin embarked on securing large paydays. He would use every willing and available contact in his network to spread his corruption throughout every level of government, from city hall to Congress. As of the writing of this book, his federal indictment is around the corner and he will likely go to prison, along with others. What disappointed me the most was coming to the understanding that, sadly, Kevin Johnson was not unique. He was not a standalone operation. In fact, mayors of many cities from Los Angeles, California, to New Haven, Connecticut were equally as greedy and corrupt as Kevin had become. Sir John Dalberg-Acton said it best when he remarked, "Power tends to corrupt, and absolute power corrupts absolutely." Indeed, with no checks and balances in place to protect the public, corruption was absolutely taking place.

Initially, the federal government only needed me to help them pursue Kevin Johnson in their investigation regarding allegations of sex trafficking and other financial crimes. However, due to jurisdictional issues, the investigation ended up pivoting to pursue him for political corruption crimes, which involved other elected officials and candidates for office, and some political action committees (PACs). Due to the sex trafficking investigating being ongoing, I am not allowed to discuss it at this time. Instead I will focus on sharing the details leading up to this current investigation. The goal of the US Attorney's Office was to indict Kevin Johnson on these initial crimes and then have him, in turn, cooperate with them to pursue many other cases. Rest assured, Special Agent Rebekah Bills, who is currently in charge of this case, is known for having a successful history of taking down sex trafficking and other deeply intertwined cases during her time at the Bureau. As the saying goes, "you can run, but you can't hide."

To give you some additional background on where Kevin Johnson and my business relationship began, after our chance meeting at a restaurant in Sacramento, California, Kevin and I almost immediately knew that we could help one another grow our net worth. It would not be until several years later in 2017, when he bought in as a shareholder of a government technology company I was involved in called Government App Solutions, formerly Text to Ticket, that he would involve many other elected politicians in his illegal activities. Founded in 2017, the company provided technology enforcement and management solutions for government agencies. The idea of Text to Ticket first came to me as a solution for cities who were struggling to enforce the new texting law. For Gov App Solutions, cities, counties, and state departments would purchase the company's technology to equip their parking and code enforcement officers with devices to capture and enforce specific violations. To secure city contracts, Kevin was calling mayors and offering them money, whether it was directly or indirectly earmarked for their next mayoral or elected position campaign, in exchange for them pushing these contracts through their city council. Oftentimes, these mayors would find ways to circumvent policies and procedures in place, like selection advisory committees, along with terminating city employees who opposed the contract to make sure the company Kevin represented secured it. This is clearly illegal.

Kevin's motivation for doing this was simple, if he could direct contracts to the company, he would not only make the company that he owned stock in more valuable, but also earn more shares of the company. If Kevin could get Government App Solutions one parking enforcement contract with an annual income of $1 million, the company's valuation could easily become $5 million to $10 million dollars. This in turn would increase the value of the shares that Kevin owned, which would increase his net worth. He could easily sell these shares or be paid out if the company were acquired down the road. For Kevin, this was an easy task given he had served as the president of the US Conference of Mayors. That position alone gave him access to virtually every mayor in the nation. He knew all of them, and he knew which ones would accept bribes and which ones he could pressure by having dirt on them.

The objective of the FBI's investigation was clear. They needed me to help them catch Kevin Johnson, on video, offering and making "quid pro quo" deals with other mayors and elected officials. On the low end, these contracts were generally worth millions of dollars. More important, these contracts were legally supposed to be put out for fair bidding from the public. However, little did individuals and small businesses know they never even had a fair chance at securing these contracts. With backdoor deals already being made, legit companies would lose tens of thousands of dollars preparing and answering these request for formal proposals (RFPs) from local governments, sometimes going broke putting everything, they had into meeting the requirements of the proposal in trying to win a contract. I have seen several companies have to close their doors after not winning the bid even though they were the most qualified.

Selling contracts to friends or the highest bidder was quite common practice for Kevin and his corrupt associates. A previous investigation into some of Kevin's associates discovered that a red-light traffic camera company called Redflex had been caught bribing city officials in return for contracts with their cities.

For those of you wondering if this is entrapment, the answer is no, without a doubt. Entrapment would require two related elements: (1) government inducement of the crime, and (2) the defendant's lack of predisposition to engage in the criminal conduct. In most of the cases in which I was involved, the government (FBI) was notified by other parties, i.e., city employees, of the elected officials ongoing crimes. The government then opened investigations to capture this illegal activity. They never asked any elected official to break the law. These elected officials voluntarily came up with their specific methods of breaking the law by offering, demanding, and accepting bribes.

In this book, I will take you on a journey of corruption that encompasses cities throughout America and to show you how the game of political power and profit is still being played. I became so good at collecting evidence in these political corruption investigations that other FBI and law enforcement departments across the nation started recruiting me for work. For me, it was a no-brainer. I understood the consequences of not doing the right thing. Aiding in this investigation would give me the chance to not only "make right" my own past crimes, but also help other communities by ending the political corruption costing millions in tax dollars and highlighting the holes in the process that don't allow for fair play. Yes, I have made mistakes. We all make mistakes; however, that does not free anyone from the consequences. In addition, there are some offenses and crimes, like sex trafficking and other crimes against people, that are unforgivable in my book. You'll read how I decided to put an end to some of the investigations conducted by the FBI, due to the fact that FBI agents were targeting certain political candidates and having me make campaign donations to help the other political party to help them win under false investigation claims.

This is the story of how some elected officials and government agencies brazenly take advantage of the system. Where is the conscience of America? I want to believe we still have one. Sit back as I explain the investigation conducted by the FBI to bring down the mighty ones once thought to be untouchable.

CHAPTER ONE
THE STORY OF ME

I could easily have been another statistic. I was raised by my mother and grandparents. No one in my family had achieved over a high school education at that time. My mother had decided to drop out of high school and worked a few jobs before landing a position for the California Department of Corrections. We moved almost every year to a new place and most of the time, due to our limited income, the neighborhoods were not the best. It was definitely not the type of environment that made it easy for children growing up to make the right choices. My brother and I were often home alone, free to run, with minimum supervision from around third grade through high school. Limited income, hours left alone, and no real adult role models was a recipe for disaster.

I'm not quite sure all of what my mother went through or who hurt her to make her such a difficult and challenging person to be around; however, I do remember going to some counseling early on and my mother being told she was bipolar. The counselor suspected other issues, but we never found out what those were. My mom was a supervisor at the Vacaville State Prison. She would supervise inmates who were on the paint crew (they would paint the prison buildings,

1

lines, etc.). The position did not require any additional schooling. She started working at the prison in the kitchen and worked her way on over to the prison grounds side. Even though she worked in law enforcement, she had difficulties communicating with us. If there was a manual on parenting back then, she would not have been the poster child. My birth father and her never got along. She had a habit of calling the police and falsely claiming he was hitting her when in actuality, she was the aggressor. These calls would put him in danger of being arrested for domestic violence, and they happened so frequently, he ended up leaving when I was in third grade. She always seemed so angry. Anyone who challenged her in any way would see her wrath. I often wondered how someone working in law enforcement could do or say the things she did. There were many times in my life when I would call law enforcement on my mother for abuse only to have the responding officers, tell me to either listen to her go to juvenile hall. It was tough and very frustrating. In the end, after decades of this behavior, she would assault a coworker, which left her only two options: retire or be fired.

As a child and teenager, I considered my mother a selfish person. She was paid a decent wage monthly, yet she had poor money management skills. She would generally run out of money after a week or two, and would not give or provide any means for lunch to my brother and me. When the food ran out and my brother and I would complain, it would always be hell to pay. She spent most of her money getting her hair done, gambling, and going out. It always felt like her priority was to find a husband, not her children.

At the age of ten, times had gotten so bad, I had to steal from my mother every month just so my brother and I would not starve. Often preoccupied with other things, she never even noticed the missing money. I devised a plan to keep food on the table. The day she was paid, I would set my alarm for midnight and crawl into my mother's room to find her purse, where she kept her entire paycheck in cash. I would go into her wallet and take $200. This would provide my brother and me with breakfast, lunch, and dinner for a while. Even though I knew this was wrong, I felt no remorse. My empty stomach and the anger I harbored for not feeling loved enough made sure of that. Often when I would voice my anger at her for being hungry, the only thing I would have to show for the confrontation were bruises from being beaten. As I grew older, the amount I would take every month from her wallet increased. Eventually we stopped asking her for anything.

The bright spots for me were my summers away from my mother when we stayed with our grandparents. Summers were a true gift from God. These were the times when I would get to see the good side of people. My grandparents demanded that we educate ourselves and give time to the Lord. It was the only stability my brother and I ever had in our lives growing up. My grandfather was a man of many successes. I loved staying with my grandparents. It was one of the few times in life I felt I could be a kid and be free. While I was younger than my brother, I was the one who took on the role of the adult growing up, but not during the summers. No checking on my older brother and watching him. No forcing him to do his homework. No having to walk to the store in the rain to buy food. I had learned to cook using the stove when I was in the third grade. In the summers, the only responsibility I had was to be a kid. I enjoyed playing with neighborhood kids, video games, Pokémon cards, and so much more. No stressing about food, electricity, lights, or abuse. Just loving grandparents. Not to say that my grandparents never spanked me . . . But when they did, I can assure you that it was well deserved.

One summer, I got especially interested in Pokémon cards. I had so many; I was a true collector. I would go to work for my grandfather almost every day to earn my keep. Once a week, my grandfather would allow me to stop at the store and spend a portion of the money I had earned that week on Pokémon cards . . . and, yes, candy. My grandfather also believed in saving for a rainy day; however, I always tried to talk him into letting me spend more of my money. It never worked. My grandfather would always say, "Spend wisely. Save. Don't put all your eggs in one basket."

One week when I made my way into the card shop to buy a few packs of cards, there were some individual Pokémon cards in a glass display for sale. They were going for $20 to over $100 per card. I was intrigued. I asked the gentleman working there why those cards were so expensive. He explained that the cards were "rare" and "valuable." I wanted to know how he knew that, and he told me they were all on a list. I asked him for a copy, and he sold it to me. I left with the store with the list in my hand and two packs of Pokémon trading cards.

As soon as I got into my grandfather's truck, he asked me what the paper was I had. I explained to him it was a list showing how much each Pokémon card was worth. He asked to see it, so I gave it to him.

He said, "Wow. Some of these could be really valuable. Do you have any of these?"

"Yes. I have a few of the higher-valued ones," I replied.

"Well, let's go back in for minute," my grandfather said.

Not understanding what he was doing, I immediately challenged him.

"I thought you said not to put all my eggs in one basket, Popo?" I asked.

"Yes. You are correct. However, today you will learn another lesson. It's called protecting your investment," he said.

When we returned to the store my grandfather brought me several sheets of card holders and a binder to put all my cards in. I was so excited! When I got home, I sat for hours organizing my cards into the page sheets, and then, of course, took count of my valuable collection. I went one by one and wrote down each card and what the value was. At the end, I had a total of just over $300 in cards already. Not bad for a fourth-grader. For two more years I continued to work so I could buy Pokémon cards and put them in my book. A simple but powerful lesson on "return on investment."

In sixth grade, my mother ended up in another one of her typical financial problems, which were becoming commonplace. There were many times where my mother would not the pay rent or bills, and she would sometimes vanish to go gamble or meet people. Nonetheless, she explained to my brother and me that we were once again going to lose our place and we would need to figure out where to live next. I loved my school and my teacher, so naturally I did not want to leave the area. My teacher was a lady named Ronda Renschler and she was truly God's gift to me. She refused to let me fail and told me that she would always be there for me. And she has been, even to this day.

When I asked my mother how much money she needed for rent, she told me $1,300. She wanted me to ask my grandparents or my godmother for help; however, I had a different plan. Armed with my Pokémon collection, it was the first time I felt more powerful than my mother. I told her I could get her the money, but there were some things I wanted in exchange. They were: take my brother and me to see the snow, take my brother and me to Hollywood Video so we could rent two video games and let us keep them for two weeks, and, lastly, I wanted her to learn how to budget and save. "Of course," she laughed and agreed. I wanted to believe her. I wanted to believe she would change.

Now she wanted to know how I was going to get the money. I told her I had some valuable cards and I could turn them into the store for money. She was infuriated. "You can't get no damn money for Pokémon cards. You're so fucking stupid. You're always trying to be one of these white people you see on TV or at school. Stop it. You'll never be anything," she yelled.

I pressed on. "Mom, please, look at this." She refused to look at my list.

I remember going to my room crying. I knew if I could just get her to the store, she would see I was telling the truth, so I came up with a plan. I would offer her money to take me! I offered her the $60 I had on me to take me to the card shop. I told her she could keep the money, regardless of the outcome. Once again, she was infuriated. She took the money and said she would get all the money in the house no matter what, and to never hide any money from her again. Upset about not being believed, I picked up the phone to call my grandparents. She attacked me and tried to hang the phone up;

however, thankfully, they picked up before she could disconnect. I could hear them yelling at her, "What are you doing?" and she offered inexcusable excuses.

"Listen to your son. He's telling you the truth," I could hear my grandfather telling her, after she told him what I'd said about the cards.

And just like that, she ushered me to the car and asked where the card shop was. At this point, I had collected over four complete copies of all the Pokémon cards and over 10 to 15 individual first-edition holographic cards, which were extremely valuable. When we got to the store, I gave the clerk my binder and told him that I would like to sell my cards. I'll never forget the look on the store owners' faces when they saw how many cards I had collected. Of course, they needed time to go through them, and I agreed to wait.

It took about half an hour to come back with an offer. While they wished they could buy more, their offer was for certain cards. The offer: $2,000. "I am rich," I thought. The man asked me what I thought, and I knew to ask for more. My grandfather taught me to always ask for more when selling and ask for a bigger discount when buying. We ended up agreeing to just over $2,100. My mother had to sign for the sale and give a copy of her ID. We left the store and grabbed ice cream next door to celebrate.

Everyone was in a good mood. We rushed home because we were heading to the snow. My mom said we could bring our game system and to pack clothes. Once in the car, she said we had to stop by my grandparents' for a minute. "Sweet!" I thought. I loved seeing my grandparents and I couldn't wait to tell my grandfather about how much money we made off my cards. I knew he would be proud of me for helping my mother. However, as I was learning, no good deed goes unpunished. My mother had a different plan in mind. Once we got to my grandparents' house, my brother and I went to the backyard to talk to my grandfather. My mother then gave $40 to my grandmother and told her we could get two video games. With that, she left.

My mother ended up going to Reno, gambling all the money away, and not coming back to get us for days. I hated my mother. I couldn't understand why or how she could do what she did. I had done the right thing by trying to help her, but again, I was lied to. When she finally showed up at my grandparents to pick us up, I let her have it. Angry that I would challenge her, she began to beat me; however, my grandparents stepped in and stopped her.

They yelled, "What were you thinking? Are you crazy? You are wrong for what you did!"

My mom screamed back what she always said, "You're not their parents. You're just trying to take my kids away from me." She then demanded my brother and I get into the car. Later that night, as we arrived home, I jumped out of the car first to head in and rush to my room. However, as I got to the front door, I was confronted by a red notice on the door. We were being evicted. Not only did my mom steal the money I had earned from the sale of my Pokémon cards, she had not even paid the rent with it.

This was normal for my mom—completely irrational behavior. I was so angry with her that I decided I would take my money back on her next payday. Due to my mother's poor management skills and being reported to the ChexSystems so many times, she did not have a bank account. So, she had to cash her check every month and keep the funds on her personally. When that day came, I ended up taking 20 one-hundred-dollar bills from her wallet. Knowing there was no way she wouldn't notice the missing money, I was prepared for what was coming. After taking the money, I left the house in the middle of the night to go to my best friend's house, where I hid the money in his front yard. I picked out a safe spot, put the money in a sandwich bag that I had placed in a metal coffee travel mug, and buried it. When we woke up in the morning, I approached my mother.

"Mom. Can I talk to you?" I asked.

"What?" she said.

"Are you going to pay me back the money that you took from me from my Pokémon cards?" I asked.

"You'd better get out of my face before you get it," she threatened.

Well, now was the time when the rubber meets the road. My anger took control of me.

"Well, I figured that you would not. You are a liar and a selfish woman. You fight my brother and me when we ask for food and simple things. Well, you should know I do not trust you. You should also know I took my money back last night. You can do what you want to me, but I'll never give it back." I couldn't believe I was able to say all of that without her lunging at me.

As quickly as the thoughts ran through my head, she jumped up and ran to her room to check her wallet. She came out yelling, and, boy, did I brace myself. The entire incident lasted only a few minutes; however, I had to distract her from going after my brother.

"He didn't know. It was only me, stupid," I said, knowing this would distract her and draw her attention back to me. However, my brother did know.

I was bleeding, sore, and bruised from her beating when she began to cry. I felt so confused. Just moments ago, I'd hated her. Now I felt extreme guilt for making her cry. The next few minutes changed my life forever.

She ran to her room and came out with a bunch of pills. Crying, she said, "Give me the money back."

"No." I said.

Just as quickly as I said no, she poured all the pills into her hands and swallowed them. She began to violently shake and fell to the ground. My brother and I lost our minds. We cried as we watched our mother lay on the floor. Not knowing what to do, I panicked. I thought that I was going to go to jail for causing my mother to kill herself. I went into her bathroom and grabbed all the pill bottles that I could. As my brother came in frantically, he asked me what I was doing. I told him I was going to take all of these pills because I did not want to go to jail. We sat there in our mothers' room trying to open the pill bottles. Thankfully, due to the child safety locks on them, we were unable to. We cried there on the bathroom floor until we fell asleep. Later, we were awakened by a friend of my mother's. After telling us to go to our room, she came in to tell us our grandparents would be there to get us in an hour, and to pack all our things. She then left. I went out to look at my mother's body. However, it was gone. I was confused and sad.

When we saw our grandparents, we ran into their arms and cried.

"What happened?" they asked. "Did you actually see it?"

My grandfather took hold of the conversation, and somehow gave light to my brother and me. "How would you guys like to live with Momo and me?" I felt relieved but the guilt would remain even after we moved in with my grandparents and started school there. My brother and I went a long time carrying that guilt. I'll never forget the day we learned she had staged everything. She had not killed herself. She apologized and said she had been working on becoming a better person, which seemed like "fluff" to me. I did not believe her.

Before my mother had staged her own death, I'd tried to tell her that a babysitter we had was a bad person. For almost a year, I was being molested by a grown woman almost daily. I would tell my mom the things she was doing to me; however, for my mom, the price the babysitter charged was too good to pass. To give her some credit, I truly think my mother was so set in her own ways that she really did not understand what I was trying to tell her. I finally stopped trying.

Ever since I can remember, I felt compelled to take care of my brother, even though he is older. He was the physical protector; however, I was the one who made sure we survived. Whenever the babysitter tried to call my brother into the back room, I would immediately get up and try to go into the room to talk to her. I did not want her touching my brother. Eventually she would send my brother back into the living room and move on to me. I would tell myself that it was okay. I had to make sure my brother was all right. I figured I was already hurt, so why should I let him get hurt. Thankfully, my mother would end up losing that apartment and causing us to move to another city far away from the babysitter. My brother and I were back on our own again; watching each other.

Through most of my teens, I would teeter back and forth from being in trouble to trying to stay clear of it as best I could. At the age of 14, I had joined the Fairfield Police Department as a volunteer police cadet and tried to tailor my life after those of my peers in the program. To become a volunteer, I had to pass a background check, my grades had to be adequate, and I had to pass physical agility test. The program served as a stability and constant in my life at that time. I loved it and spent all my free time volunteering there.

My grandparents lived in Fairfield, California, however, I ended up living in Elk Grove, California, with my mother and brother. The city had just opened a new school with great teachers, opportunities, and computer courses, which I had a great interest in.

Fortunately, I settled into school and was dating my high school crush. Life was finally starting to seem normal. However, that did not last long. Once again, we were being evicted because of my mother's gambling and money mismanagement skills. We had to move back in with my grandparents, which made no sense because in reality, my mother had a good and stable job. There should have been no reason that she couldn't maintain her monthly financial obligations. This time I was determined not to lose the sense of normalcy we had finally come to experience, but I didn't know what to do. Fortunately, my mother found out she could not transfer my brother and I so late in the year to one of the schools in Fairfield, so she had to take us to school in Elk Grove every morning. We had a Mazda RX7, a two-seater car, and I had to generally ride in the trunk for the one-hour drive.

Eventually, the commute would take its toll on my mother. She told us we needed to get jobs to help pay the bills instead of going to school. I asked if I could arrange for my own transportation back and forth to school, would she allow me to continue with school? She agreed; however, I couldn't find anyone to give me a ride. I was desperate to stay in school. Being that I was volunteering as a cadet for the police department, I had access to the volunteer vehicles. There were a few problems with my logic: I was the youngest cadet, I had no license, and more important, it would be theft. That was illegal. Yet, I was determined not to drop out of school and lose my chance at an education. Not knowing how to drive, I had to teach myself in a crash course, over a weekend. And so, it began. Every morning I would go to the police department, grab the keys to one of the volunteer vehicles, and drive to Elk Grove, California, for school. I would attend school and then head back to Fairfield and return the car. This happened for several months until one morning, I got caught. Our school campus officer got suspicious and tried to run my information to verify if I had a driver's license. After no luck, he decided to contact the department and ask why they were letting me use a department car to go to and from school.

In the end, I would end up being arrested and going to juvenile hall. The court granted me a deferred entry of judgment (DEJ). It was a program that would allow me to leave juvenile hall immediately, require me to participate in a program while on probation, and then the incident would be removed from my record. I would like to say that this was the first and last time I would encounter law enforcement and the court system, however, that is not how my story goes. After getting arrested, I remember my mother being happy about it. Ever since I could remember, she never really advocated for me. She would put me down, calling me "white-washed" whenever I had the opportunity to better myself. She was physically and mentally abusive to me. When she was not abusing me, she was fine with letting someone else abuse me as long as the situation suited her.

Unfortunately, I would then end up experiencing sexual abuse again in my high school years, this time by a powerful and wealthy lady. She would end up blackmailing me, until I refused to cooperate anymore. It was not long until I was arrested and prosecuted. The DA had no interest in pursuing or hearing about her sexual misconduct. All in all, I learned very early to not trust people. I learned that without proof of abuse, of being molested, no one believed you. If only I could have captured all of it on video, I would have been believed then. However, having been arrested in the past, any time a situation came down to me versus someone else's truth, I was always wrong. It was that simple. Because I had broken the law before, I was the one who continued to pay the price. It was a merry-go-round I wanted so badly to get off of. Moving forward, I told myself that any time I felt like things could go wrong, I would record the events and save them just in case. I was the only one looking out for me. Little did I know this change in mindset would come in handy later in my life.

CHAPTER TWO
ENTREPRENEUR AT HEART

Despite all the trouble that I got into and the challenges that I faced when I was younger, I actually went on to pursue higher education after high school, enrolling in National Paralegal College, becoming the first in my family to earn a degree. From there, I enrolled in another college, University of Phoenix, to pursue my second degree in business.

Throughout my twenties and early thirties, I started and sold several companies successfully. I even became a speaker at Stanford Law School for legal technology.[1] Between the years 2014 and 2017, I had become known in the startup world for creating a company called Quicklegal. My team and I entered a California app competition and won first place for creating the best app of the year at Techweek.[2] Who would have ever thought that could happen to a young black felon?

One of the companies I started was a company called California Legal Pros. It was a company that provided self-help legal and paralegal services to law firms and attorneys. One of the more popular services was the unlawful detainer package for property owners. If they were having trouble getting their tenants out of their property due to unpaid rent, destroying the property, or other lease violations, they would hire us to evict them. I started this company for about $3,000 in 2012. It quickly grew to become one of the largest unlawful detainer companies in California. I expanded and had several offices in a matter of two years.

In 2014, during the last year of my ownership in California Legal Pros, I became aware of some inconsistent revenue at one of the branches. At the time, I had hired a friend I met in prison to work for me. He, unfortunately, lost his way and began charging and stealing money from a client of ours. When I found out about this, I immediately confronted him. He explained to me that this particular client was horrible and racist, and that he was disgusted by it. After hearing some of the voicemails and reading some of the email correspondence, I wrongfully turned a blind eye.

After several months, the client continued to pay more and more money. I was now part of the scheme. The client was under the impression that he had been fined by the court, and he needed to take care of this due to the condition of the home he had rented to his tenants.

While on social media one day, I saw the client who had been defrauded in my company on my suggested friends list. Of course, my curiosity got me, and I clicked on the profile to see the client. I was almost immediately disturbed. I could tell by some of the images on the profile page that the wife was having some sort of medical challenge, and it appeared the family was trying to do an online campaign to raise money. I was disgusted with what I had done. I had lost my way.

For the next several days, I spent time going over what had happened, and, more importantly, why I had not only allowed it, but taken part in the scheme. I was questioning myself and trying to figure out how I had gotten so far off course. I knew something had to change. I knew that I had to do something to fix this situation. I needed to get back on the right path. I decided to write the client an email and tell him that the court had reversed all fines and orders, and that he would be receiving his money back.

I had also decided that it was time to sell that company. It was mid-2014, and I'd had the company for just over two years now. I no longer wanted it, as it reminded me of the guilt I held for my wrongful actions. I talked to a business broker about selling the company. It just so happened that she had been contacted by another broker looking for a legal services business like mine. So, I decided to move forward and explore this option.

Several weeks later, I had a solid deal with a buyer who happened to be a licensed California attorney who'd graduated from Harvard Law School. A company that I had started just two years prior, for a few thousand dollars, was now being sold for several hundred thousand dollars. It was exciting.

To celebrate, I treated my employees to a late lunch at an upscale restaurant in the downtown Sacramento area.

I rose to give a toast to the staff for a job well done. We all cheered.

Out of the corner of my eye, I saw a tall man watching me as I spoke. He was former National Basketball Association (NBA) basketball player and superstar Kevin Johnson, who was then the mayor of Sacramento.

After my toast, a woman from the mayor's team approached me and asked if the mayor could have a minute of my time. I walked over and introduced myself.

"I couldn't help but overhear your conversation," Kevin said. "Are you the manager of the company?"

"No, I'm the owner of this company," I said. I explained to him what the company did.

"What kind of revenue are you bringing in?" he asked.

"We do anywhere from $20,000 a month to $60,000 a month," I replied.

"And you're the only owner?" he pried. I nodded.

"We've got to get to know each other," Kevin said.

For me, this was a great opportunity. Being a younger African-American with a criminal past, my business associates were limited. However, if a mayor and former NBA superstar was taking me under his wing, that would be a game changer. So, we began hanging out. Yet, my focus at that time was selling my company.

In late 2014, I closed escrow on the sale of California Legal Pros and started a new company called Quicklegal. I envisioned this company to help average people have immediate access to licensed attorneys throughout the nation. They could instantly video chat with an attorney or submit a legal question, which a licensed attorney would respond to.

We were showing early signs of success. We got accepted in a top incubator and accelerator program called 500 Startups, which invested over $125,000 into the company and raised my company valuation to just over $2.5 million. On top of that, this program was known as the best in Silicon Valley. It was the Stanford of these types of programs. It had an acceptance rate of less than 1 percent.

As time progressed, Quicklegal grew. We won competition after competition, were featured in the national news, raised money from investors, and bridged the gap between law and technology. Then came an exciting time. A major legal company called LegalZoom was interested in us. It wanted us to terminate our relationship with Rocket Lawyer (LegalZoom's competition) and just do business with LegalZoom. After several months of due diligence and planning, LegalZoom said it wanted to acquire the company. This was huge. Especially because Quicklegal was valued somewhere between $10 million and $15 million.

However, my past would come up to haunt me. My former client, who I had emailed and told there had been a mistake and he would be getting his money back, got suspicious after receiving the email. Several weeks later, he went to the court and found out that none of the information he had been given was true. So, during the months that I was building Quicklegal, he had hired an attorney and was building a lawsuit to sue me and my company.

One day, I was pulling up to my house and there was a process server walking away from my front door. I called for his attention and he asked me if I was Derek Bluford. I said, "Yes," of course, and accepted service. As soon as I pulled out the papers and saw the client name on the lawsuit, I went numb.

After a day or two, I knew what I had needed to do. I had to continue to make this situation right and take full responsibility. I immediately waived the trial and agreed to a court judgment for whatever monetary damages were requested.

Once the lawsuit and settlement was finalized, a legal blogger got wind of it and wrote an article about me and the lawsuit. It was not long until other publications were also starting to write about it. When the board of directors of Quicklegal became aware of the news, they wanted answers. I stood before the board, gave the directors the truth, and then resigned.

LegalZoom had backed out of the acquisition, and, oddly enough, connected with the first blogger to state that they had no business with me or Quicklegal at all. Such a bold statement, especially knowing that they had sent me and others on my team emails, legal agreements, and more. Nonetheless, I had bigger problems to deal with.

I was now being contacted by attorneys left and right regarding litigation complaints for putting the shareholders of Quicklegal in a bad position. I was having to pay and offer settlements to these shareholders in return for them not suing me. My finances were declining rapidly, and I had nothing coming in to offset it.

I knew that I needed to get a job or start a new company to generate income. During this time, Kevin Johnson and I were building our relationship even more. Ironically, I was not the only one being publicly written about. Journalists were often writing about Kevin Johnson, and accusations were popping up and being whispered around city hall. He would often tell me not to worry about it. He would say that lawsuits and mistakes are a part of business and growing. He told me that he could get me a job at the city or working for one of his friends. However, I was too embarrassed to show my face in public while journalists were still writing about my foolish mistakes. So, I started a Web development company.

As Kevin and I began to take a more public approach with our friendship, mutual friends of ours would pull me to the side and warn me about him. They would say, "Watch your back. Be careful." They warned me that Kevin was a professional blackmailer. However, I did not have many choices, and the potential benefits of access outweighed the risks, which I could plan for. After all, if someone were to look me up online, they would be hesitant to do any kind of business with me, given the recent articles. Yet, when a superstar mayor was signing off on me, saying there was no choice and to just get it done, that was a big game changer—one that I had desperately needed.

Nonetheless, my earlier experiences in life had taught me to always protect myself, just in case. I thought it would be wise to track everything with Kevin. Even before I started working undercover for the FBI, I would usually wear or have a hidden digital recorder or a camera pen. I knew this was illegal in the state of California; however, I knew I should not take any chances participating in activities that sounded like they were not on the up and up. I figured, if our relationship ever soured and he were to throw me under the bus for something, who would they believe—the mayor of Sacramento or me?

So, I decided to record any illegal activities as a backup. After all, it was Kevin Johnson that I was dealing with, and he was well connected. It was reported in a Sacramento newspaper that "He's just a person with money that can buy himself into safety."[3] He was friends with the chief of police. He had dirt on the sheriff, on prosecutors, and all the way to the top. If someone ever tried to bring him down, they would immediately be cut off with attacks from the top and the bottom. That was how far his hands and his favors went.

However, again, for someone in my shoes, he provided a lot of opportunity for me to better my life. From introductions to celebrities—such as Jesse Jackson, Al Sharpton, Barry Bonds and more—to directing investors to come onboard one of my ventures, to even getting the local police department to help out with favors here and there, Kevin did prove to be useful at times. Floor seats came along with meet-and-greets with NBA players and included fine dining. Kevin provided access to it all.

One day Kevin said to me, "Hey, D, is Quicklegal looking for partners or anything like that? I noticed you aren't signed up with the city as a vendor."

Although I had resigned from Quicklegal, I was still the majority shareholder of the company, and therefore, had its best interest in mind. On top of that, after my resignation, the board of directors called me back to become a consultant for the company and paid me for more app and Web development services.

I told Kevin no, that Quicklegal was not signed up as a city vendor, and that most of what Quicklegal was focusing on was technology, although it still had a department that focused on providing services to landlords.

"Well, you know the city is a landlord," Kevin said.

I did.

However, before Kevin could pursue the corrupt opportunity, about March 2016, he was back in the spotlight as national news networks were starting to talk about a documentary being produced that would have several of his sexual assault victims in it.

In April 2016, Kevin chose me to be a speaker at the Sacramento BizX conference. It was a high-profile, local business event and reminded me of the value of having a mayor as a friend. That is when Kevin introduced me to US Congresswoman Doris Matsui, who was also speaking and participating at the event.

But as always with Kevin, there was an ask.

"Hey, D, after you are done presenting, I want you to meet up with me."

I did, and he asked me how the presentation went. I said I enjoyed it.

"I need your help," Kevin said. "We're going to be proposing some stuff at city council and some people are going to be objecting to it. You are a small business guy. If you could be at the hearing to support it, that would be great. Here is some material. Take a look at it and let me know what you think."

It was a script supporting the proposed city funding program. He advised me to rehearse it before the meeting. He asked me if I was "cool" with it and I said, "Yes." He also said not to worry, because he and a few city council members had some other local business owners onboard who would also be helping them out. He said that it was a "numbers game" and that they would make sure that they got more public speakers during the city council meeting in favor of the program than those who opposed it. Little did I know this artificial "lobbying" of the city council would become a regular thing for me and many other local business owners. City council members and Mayor Johnson would write scripts, issue them, and then reward us with grants, sporting game tickets, money, and other incentives.

Members of the public who saw us speaking at city council meetings had no idea that our support was staged and had been scripted by the mayor, his staff, and other city council members. People cannot even trust public hearings to be honest and aboveboard. Often, they are not. And there was a system of rewards and punishments to enforce this game.

Business owners who publicly supported the mayor and some of the city council's initiatives were rewarded with grants, great business opportunities, quick building permit approvals, and more. On the other hand, if people did not go along with the city, they would often find themselves facing targeted retaliation. As a business owner, these punishments could range from having issues with business licenses and permits to customers getting parking tickets to, suddenly, neighbors showing up at city council meetings complaining that the business was disruptive to the neighborhood. That was all directed by Kevin Johnson and some city council members.

For example, there was a developer by the name of Paul Petrovich who was not getting onboard with what Mayor Kevin Johnson and other corrupt city council members were demanding from him. So, they shut him down, blocked his development plan, and cost him tens of millions of dollars. Just like that. Petrovich s 72-acre development of brownstone homes, a shopping center, and apartments were no longer happening.[4]

In June 2016, Kevin and the Sacramento City Council created the Rapid Acceleration, Innovation, and Leadership (RAILS) program in Sacramento. It provided grants to local businesses. Kevin brought in a specialist as an independent contractor who had expertise in raising capital, government technology, and improving municipalities. The guy was brilliant, yet unaware of Kevin's plan to defraud the public and direct the flow of most of the grants, with some of his corrupt city council members, to businesses that had already struck backdoor deals with them.

Kevin's pitch to the public, other mayors, and businesses was that they needed to become a smart city 3.0 (a concept to balance the past and the future of a community while improving quality of life through technology). He was always speaking to mayors about improving their cities and forming potential partnerships. Unfortunately, Kevin always tried to milk money out of them.

If mayors were facing a challenge in their cities or needed help with a voting issue, Kevin would charge them money behind closed doors. In return, he could get celebrity access and public endorsements from other mayors. Nonetheless, Kevin was a great storyteller. He could make people believe. Most of his speeches made sense, and he could always make them relate to the audience. At the 82nd United States Conference of Mayors, Kevin gave the following speech regarding 3.0 cities.

Today, we are entering the era of Cities 3.0. In this era, the city is a hub of innovation, entrepreneurship and technology. It's paperless, wireless, and cashless. In 3.0 cities we have more cell phones than landlines, more tablets than desktops and more smart devices than toothbrushes. This truly represents a new era of the American city. And what is the role of the mayor in the 3.0 city?

The 3.0 city must be the "ultimate service provider." Why? Because 3.0 citizens operate in a new paradigm. In this generation, the world's largest music company has no record stores (Apple). The world's largest bookseller has no bookstores (Amazon). The world's largest taxi company has no cars (Uber). It's only a matter of time before the world's largest hotel will have no hotel rooms (AirBnB). And soon, the world's largest university will have no campus. That means we need to provide city services on new platforms too.

In Cities 2.0, city crews would drive around looking for reported potholes to fill them. It could take weeks or months for a response. In Cities 3.0 here's what it would look like: That pothole on my street? I should be able to take a picture of it with my phone and upload it through a city app that will tag it with its GPS location. Providers throughout the city could instantaneously be dispatched to fill the pothole on the same day. It's quicker, easier and more efficient. And active, connected citizens become part of the city's network to solve problems.[5]

However, as always, it was an opportunity for Kevin. If he could get the RAILS grant program approved, it would be a win for the city and, more important, a win for him. Kevin knew most of the companies in Sacramento. If they wanted a grant from the city, there would be a price to pay, behind closed doors, of course. It was always a chess game.

Kevin originally told the public that his goal was to raise $1 million from investors to fund the program. However, he knew that he had much more than that already committed. That is how he would set up his "accomplishments." He would, in theory, rig the game or set the story, saying, "If only we can reach $1 million," knowing that he had already raised $6 million. In the end, he raised about $10 million, a huge win for him.

Kevin always tried to stage these wins for himself to build up momentum for his "strong mayor" campaign. The City of Sacramento currently stood as a "weak mayor" system, meaning that most big decisions had to be voted on by the city council. Most cities are characterized as having either a "weak" or a "strong" mayor system. The term is not a judgment, instead it distinguishes the level of political power and administrative authority assigned to the mayor. Although, when Kevin pushed for a vote to become a "strong" mayor and lost, he thought that he would continue to build the momentum for his next round, in case he changed his mind to run for another term.

Kevin believed that the RAILS program could personally net him a couple of million dollars in kickbacks from the companies that he granted and awarded the grants to. Even though there was a board that was supposed to review and approve the applications for RAILS grants, most of the board members were under the direction of Kevin.

I know this because Kevin and another city council member offered me the same deal. To provide comfort and assurance, they had disclosed a few other people and companies that were already on board. They told me that I could get one of the $250,000 grants toward one of my companies. However, I knew better. I knew that Kevin had been investigated several times for fraud when it came to grants that he either received or oversaw. I knew that people would be paying attention to him and these grants. I did not need any more bad press, and I thought that I was potentially under investigation myself for my crime several years ago.

The RAILS grants were supposed to go to local businesses, up for fair competition. Some did, but most did not. Kevin and some members of the city council (not all . . . there were some clean city council members) and members of the independent review panel struck deals with companies for these grants in exchange for money, kickbacks, business opportunities, and sometimes in the form of ownership interests in the companies. Two of the city council members met with Kevin and participated in these schemes. They and other officials, who were the ones deciding which companies received grants, were either paid by some of the grant applicants or received favors that would relate to employment, issuance of stock, and other benefits.

However, Kevin wanted to make this a big win, because he knew it would be one of his last, at least while at city hall. Over the course of the year, Kevin's past sexual allegations, victims, and more recent claims from new victims were beginning to constantly hit the media. He had decided in October 2015 to not seek another term after his mayoral term ended in 2016.

Kevin tried to balance the negative media with positive stories and successes he was claiming. He was meeting with President-elect Donald Trump at Trump's golf club in New Jersey and focusing on underserved communities.

Kevin's wife, Michelle Rhee, a former DC school superintendent, was interviewing for US Secretary of Education. It made sense that Trump was considering Michelle for the post. She was an avid advocate for charter schools. But it was an odd appearance for Kevin, a confirmed Democrat and a big Hillary Clinton supporter.

People were always amazed. How could Kevin Johnson so easily walk into these places, have these powerful connections, and be praised as the great one? Not only was there the 15-year-old girl (Mandi Koba) incident, but several more that followed. Sexual allegations would resurface again publicly at St. HOPE Academy, the charter school Kevin and Michelle established in Sacramento. Kevin was principal of the school before he was elected mayor of Sacramento.

A federal investigation found that Michelle, a board member of St. HOPE, was a "fixer" to clean up Kevin's mistakes. A teenager at the school alleged that Kevin had "inappropriately touched her." A school staff member duly reported the allegations to the school's human resources department, but later resigned to protest what she described as a coverup by the school.

There were many other problems at St. HOPE, according to federal investigators. Federal grants that were supposed to be used for tutors were instead used by Kevin to hire people to "wash his car [and] run personal errands,"[6] the investigation found.

Sexual scandal followed Kevin to Sacramento City Hall when he became mayor. In 2015, a former employee of the Sacramento city manager's office complained that Kevin had called her into his private library in city hall in December 2013 and gave her "an unwelcome and close hug." He "felt along her torso"[7] and tried to kiss her, then proposed they begin a sexual relationship, even though she had pushed him away and told him she was married.

More importantly, Kevin was being forced to talk about these matters in press conferences because he was the mayor. Kevin decided that he did not want to run for mayor again. As Kevin's term was ending, we discussed the exit play. He wanted to tell the people of Sacramento that he had made the city better, brought a lot of opportunities, and now wanted to pursue other paths.

He wanted me to give him a major gift in front of everyone at city hall, during the last public meeting. It was a Muhammad Ali boxing glove, signed by Muhammad Ali. Kevin provided me a script and asked me to present the gift and speech to him during the last meeting. Kevin wanted me to emphasize how Ali was a great fighter and how Mayor Kevin Johnson was also a great fighter for the City of Sacramento. We did just that. The crowd was amazed and shocked that such a gift was being given. Everyone came up to see it. That is how it always worked with Kevin. It was always a show, and he was always the director. After, Kevin wanted to cover his tracks. We met up after this, and he wanted to send me an email thanking me, and have me respond in front of him. Kevin always knew how to cover his tracks.

I was sticking around because Kevin was introducing me to powerful, big-name people. It was always beneficial to me, my companies, and, more importantly, rebuilding my reputation. On the other hand, I was introducing him to startup companies that I was involved in. When I introduced him to a government technology company I was involved in, he would soon teach me the world of dirty politics. Having controlled the machinery of a major American city, including some in the police department, business ecosystem, politics, and the judicial system, Kevin knew how to make things work in his circle of corrupt officials.

More importantly, he was looking past all the noise regarding my poor decisions; at least that is what I thought initially. In fact, Kevin was just looking for someone who was willing to compromise their ethics and morals and break laws with him to get richer. However, I was always paranoid because I knew that I was still within the statute of limitations for prosecutors to bring a case against me for the crime that had been committed against my client back in 2014.

Then, the invoice became due. On January 17, 2018, federal agents showed up at my residence to arrest me. The morning they came to get me, I was so relieved. The stress of not knowing if I would ever be charged for the crime against my client and having to wait for the other shoe to drop was finally over. (The first shoe was the civil suit.)

I remember the shocked look on the law enforcement officials' faces when I said, "Boy, am I happy to see you guys." They were confused and saddened by my enthusiasm for their presence. I told them I was not interested in fighting the charges. I had made a mistake. I had profited from it. I was wrong. "Go ahead and get this over with." I did not want to challenge or fight anything costing the people more money . . . I simply wanted to hurry up and get it over with. However, they had a different plan.

CHAPTER THREE

THE FBI

The morning I was indicted, I was released the same day on $50,000 bail. The terms of my release were (1) I had to obey all laws; (2) I had to participate in moral reconation therapy (MRT), a cognitive behavioral treatment approach; and (3) I could not be employed by or provide any legal services during the course of this case.

Over the next few days, the US Attorney's Office would request that my counsel and three alternative attorneys not be able to represent me in my case, due to a potential conflict of interest. So, in turn, the court appointed a federal defender for me.

During this time, I also began to participate in the MRT program, which was led by a woman named Tai. She was an officer of the court, non-bullshitter, and authentic. In a weird way, it was refreshing. She, oddly enough, knew me better than I knew myself. She had every piece of information on me that was ever recorded, from my current case, text messages, emails, everything all the way back to when I was born and issued a birth certificate.

Her goal was to help me change the way of my thinking. The MRT program was like that of an Alcoholics Anonymous (AA) program.

There are 12 steps to practice, and failure was not an option. If I failed this program or got on her wrong side, she could have me in jail within the hour.

Shortly after this, the US Attorney's Office and my attorney were discussing a proposed resolution for my case and scheduled a meeting for all of us to get together.

After arriving at the US Attorney's Office, my attorney reminded me to not say anything unless he told me to. He said to let the assistant US attorney (AUSA) do all the talking. After passing through security and checking in, the AUSA who was prosecuting me came and collected my attorney and I from the lobby. His name was Todd Pickles. He was oddly nice and professional toward me. As he led us down the hall, I saw the main agent, who had just arrested me at my house not long ago, walking up.

"Hi, Mr. Bluford. How are you doing?" she said as she stuck out her hand to shake mine.

"Hi." I reached out to shake her hand.

What is going on? I thought. *They are being awfully nice to me.* However, in just a few minutes I was about to find out why.

After shaking hands, they proceeded to walk my attorney and I into a conference room. As soon as we entered the conference room, we knew this would be an interesting meeting. Waiting in the room were several people. It is fair to say that both my attorney and I were caught off guard. We looked at each other and said, "What is going on?"

AUSA Todd Pickles said, "Please take your seats. We have some questions for you."

As we were seated, my attorney said, "Mr. Pickles, before we move forward, I am going to need some context here. We were under the impression that this was going to be friendly meeting."

"It is. First, we appreciate Mr. Bluford agreeing to meet with us today. It's my understanding that Mr. Bluford is aware of his charges and does not want to contest them. In fact, I believe Mr. Bluford is relieved to get this mistake over and done with," said AUSA Pickles.

"That's correct. Might I ask why the room seems so full?" asked my attorney.

"Well, we would like to talk to Mr. Bluford about his crime, and then ask him about others that he might or might not know about. In return, I believe we can help Mr. Bluford wrap up his case, by asking the court to reduce his sentence," said AUSA Pickles.

"Meaning?" asked my attorney

"Meaning if Mr. Bluford is cooperative with us, then we would ask the court or perhaps make a recommendation to the court in regards to Mr. Bluford's sentence. It could be anywhere from half off to probation," said AUSA Pickles.

"All right. There is obviously more going on than what we had planned for today. So, if you could do me a favor and walk us through what this meeting would look like if it were to be successful for you, that would help us a lot," said my attorney.

"For obvious reasons, I can't be too direct, at least not right now. It's also going to take a joint effort on behalf of Mr. Bluford. I can say though, if Mr. Bluford is willing to answer some questions of ours here today and agree to enter into a proffer and cooperation agreement, that this mistake of his can be dealt with more quickly. Mr. Bluford will be able to return to his life in a rather quick fashion," said AUSA Pickles.

Everyone then looked at me.

"Okay. Yes," I said.

"Mr. Bluford, to be clear, and before we start, I must give you some ground rules. Joining us today are several federal agents from different law enforcement branches under the Department of Justice. Therefore, anything you say must be the truth, because if you mislead or lie to us, that is a federal crime. Do you understand this?" said AUSA Pickles.

"I do."

"Great. To start off, why don't you walk us through your crime as it relates to your client who was defrauded? This will set the ground for us moving forward. Please be clear and honest. Half-truths are and will be considered a lie," said AUSA Pickles.

This was easy for me. My crime had been a constant nightmare for me over the past few years. It often played over and over in my head night after night. And when I was not dreaming about it, people were asking me about it. I would always have someone saying, "Derek, are you okay? I heard . . ."

Over the course of the next hour or two, I explained to them my crime and how it had played out. I told them that at the end, it needed to be me who took full responsibility for everything. Between my explanations, they would ask me questions they already had the answers to, and I would answer them correctly.

After answering all their questions regarding my case, they all looked at one another and gave facial expressions that indicated, "I am satisfied with this." However, Todd Pickles voiced it and said, "Does anybody else have any other questions?" No one did.

"Mr. Bluford, do you need any water or a restroom break before we move on?" said AUSA Pickles.

"No," I said. When, in fact, I did. I was just so damn nervous, embarrassed, and stressed that I literally felt numb.

Then it finally came down to the moment that we were all truly there for.

"Mr. Bluford, do you know Kevin Johnson?" said AUSA Pickles.

"As in the former mayor?" I asked.

"Yes," said AUSA Pickles.

"Yes. I do," I replied.

"Okay. Now comes the fun part. As I mentioned earlier, there are several agents from different law enforcement branches under the Department of Justice here. They are going to ask you some basic questions. Depending on those answers, they will either want to meet with you again or not. Let me now remind you that anything you say must be the full truth. If you are dishonest, even about the littlest thing, we will no longer be willing to help you and all bets are off. Okay?" said AUSA Pickles.

"I understand," I said.

"Hello, Mr. Bluford. I am Special Agent Reggie Coleman with the FBI. How are you doing?"

"I am okay."

"I know that this meeting has been going a little longer than you anticipated, so I am going to try to be direct and quick," said Special Agent Coleman.

"Okay."

"Are you aware of any illegal activities that former Mayor Kevin Johnson has committed? Whether it involves crimes from when he was in office, after he left office, or now?"

Now this was a tricky question. Was I aware of any illegal activities? Well, yes. Had I participated in any . . . well, yes to that also. I sat there for a moment contemplating this question. Then my conscience kicked in again. I was happy to be here. It was time to pay for everything that I had done wrong. I needed to be honest and just get this all over with.

"Yes," I told them.

Now, my attorney should have halted this meeting and asked that a proffer and cooperation agreement be signed immediately. However, as per usual, he was an overworked public attorney, and I believe he was just as interested in the answers to these questions, too.

"Are you aware of the sexual allegations that have been made against Mr. Johnson by several victims?" asked Special Agent Coleman.

"Yes. I am aware of them," I said.

"You seem like a good guy who lost his way. I know that you basically told on yourself in regard to your crime, and that you have been waiting to get this over with. If I were to share some evidence with you showing that Mr. Johnson was, in fact, guilty of those crimes, and also possibly sex trafficking of minors, would you consider helping the FBI catch Mr. Johnson for many crimes that we believe he is involved in? After all, you were a victim of this yourself when you were a kid. I would think that you would have many reasons to try and help us on this. But I could be wrong. Would you?" asked Special Agent Coleman.

This was true. I had always thought the allegations were just that and had no weight until one night at Kevin's home when he made a comment. I knew this was something that I could do that would have real meaning.

"Yes."

"Great. Now, if you do not mind, Mr. Bluford, can you give us all a few minutes and then we will come get you once we are ready to continue?" asked Special Agent Coleman.

"Yes," I said again.

My attorney and I then stepped out into the hallway, and I felt like that was the first time in two hours that I was able to breathe. I was drenched in my own sweat. My attorney was a little shocked that I even knew that mayor. He asked me, "Are there any other politicians you know?" Yes. Definitely, yes. It was only a few minutes until AUSA Pickles came and got us.

"Okay. We are ready for you. Sorry about that," said AUSA Pickles.

We headed back into the room. Special Agent Coleman said that they would like to have me come out to the FBI office to continue this meeting later.

I agreed to do so.

CHAPTER FOUR
THE PROMISE THAT FAILED

W ithout a doubt, Kevin Johnson was a great basketball player—even a superstar. In the history of the NBA, no other player has averaged at least 20 points, ten assists, a .516 field goal percentage, with 2.1 steals per game in a single season. Kevin achieved this during just one season in 1990–1991.

He was a consistently great player, not just a one-season sensation. Kevin was one of only four players in NBA history to average at least 20 points and ten assists per game in three different seasons. His list of records goes on. Kevin made the NBA All-Star team three times. When he retired, the Phoenix Suns retired his number 7, a sign of true greatness.

Kevin achieved this success despite his challenging childhood. His mother was 16 when he was born; his father accidentally drowned in the Sacramento River when Kevin was three. Kevin stands about six foot one—not a tall man by NBA standards. But he was extremely quick, deft, and a great shooter. He played basketball at the University of California, Berkeley, shattering records. He was also a talented baseball player, drafted by the Oakland Athletics in 1986, but he chose basketball instead.

After retiring from sports in 2000, Kevin was not the type to bask in his glory and spend his days on the golf course. He returned to Sacramento where he became active in business, specifically the nonprofit world, and politics. This powerful combination of non-profit and politics had the potentially to lead him to state and national office, if only Kevin had not been Kevin. In 1989, he founded St. HOPE Academy, a nonprofit organization and charter school with the ambitious goal of revitalizing low-income communities through better education, the arts, and economic development.

His achievements were marred by allegations of sex with an underage girl at the charter school. Again, police investigated but no charges were filed. A teacher who had initially reported the girl's allegations to police, resigned. "St. HOPE sought to intimidate the student through an illegal interrogation and even had the audacity to ask me to change my story,"[1] the teacher said.

Despite these controversies, Kevin was elected mayor of his hometown, Sacramento, California, in 2008. That was no small feat and no small prize. Sacramento is a city of 500,000 people and the capital of the nation's most populous state. Kevin was the city's first black mayor, elected the same year that Barack Obama was elected as the first black president of the United States.

"Obama and myself, we ran on the promise and the theme of change. No more business as usual," Johnson told the *Sacramento Bee*. "I am so ready and so humbled to accept this great honor that has been bestowed upon me today."[2]

The sad part of Kevin's story is what might have been. He had the talent, the intelligence, the charisma, and the energy to achieve truly great things. But for Kevin, greatness had a different meaning.

Everything about his mission, which he claimed was to help others, came with a price tag. That price tag was constructed to benefit him personally and financially. And that is precisely the reason his legacy would crumble.

CHAPTER FIVE
A CORRUPT SYSTEM

In 2017, I sold my app development company and started a new public safety company with others. It was my first government technology company. I would later introduce Kevin to the team. After meeting with us and seeing the business model, Kevin wanted in.

One of the main services that the company provided was to enable citizens—passengers or pedestrians, not drivers—to capture videos on their cell phones of motorists texting or talking on their mobile phones while driving. The company would then use that video evidence—which would include the license plate numbers of the vehicles—to send out traffic tickets to the violators. The citizens who submitted the pictures would be paid a small fee. The local governments would receive millions in revenue from the fines and our company would get millions in profits.

Everybody benefited except the poor driver who received a ticket in the mail for texting and driving. It was like the camera programs that caught drivers running red lights, adopted by cities across the country, which were actually operated by private companies. Our company followed the same business model.

Because Kevin was a shareholder of the company, he wanted to introduce Text To Ticket (which would later become Government App Solutions) to his network of elected officials across the country. To propose this plan to leadership, he requested a meeting with them at the office. The company was happy to have him. After all, to some he was still known as a superstar around Sacramento. However, that meeting would not go as Kevin had planned.

After quick pleasantries, Kevin got down to business.

"What if I can get you contracts throughout the nation?" Kevin asked.

"That would be great. How would you do that?" the chief executive officer (CEO) asked.

"Don't worry about that," Kevin assured. "I'll just get you guys the contracts."

Kevin had immediately caused some major concern among some of the leadership team by insinuating that he could deliver much more than just introductions.

The CEO of the company also happened to be a law enforcement officer, and immediately challenged Kevin. I'd met the CEO through mutual friends at Sonoma Raceway, where they raced sports cars. The CEO knew what Kevin was implying and immediately wanted no part of it.

"I need to know what that means. If it is something that is not above board, then don't even hint at that," the CEO told Kevin.

"No, no, not at all. I am just saying that I know mayors all over the country, and that they would love this service," Kevin said.

Kevin could not believe what he was hearing, and he immediately made up a reason to leave the meeting shortly thereafter. He texted me to stop by his house after the meeting.

"I don't know what's up with those guys," Kevin said, "but I don't need to meet with them anymore. You and I can just work together on this."

Because I was a shareholder of the company and also a cofounder, I had a lot of sway. The idea of running a legitimate company without bribing or negotiating behind closed-door deals with anyone was foreign to Kevin. But I already knew from my earlier dealings with Kevin that this was how he liked to play the game. So, Kevin and I started down that path, unbeknownst to the rest of the company executives.

"Let's start with Phoenix," Kevin said. "I will set everything up, and you can always present it to the company as if you are the one bringing the deal."

Now remember, Kevin was an NBA basketball superstar in Phoenix. That is where he had spent his glory days. The mayor, Greg Stanton, was a close friend.

"I've done so many favors for this guy, he owes me," Kevin said.

Kevin arranged a phone call with the three of us—Greg, Kevin, and me. After a quick catchup, during which Greg thanked Kevin for previous favors, Kevin said, "No problem. I need one from you. I'm part of this company and we do tickets for texting and driving." Kevin explained, "I need a contract with the city."

"Absolutely," Stanton said. "Send them my way. Send me information on my personal email." (The personal email would be used to avoid public scrutiny.)

Kevin and I both wrote it down.

"Yeah, have them send over the information and we'll get going. This is going to need to be quick though, as I plan on running for Congress soon," Stanton said.

The pressure was on. I immediately went back to the office and started putting the material together to send off. I sent the introductory email to his personal email, but also copied his work email, as this was just out of habit to ensure that one of his staff members would also receive it, in case Stanton did not.

That prompted an immediate call from Kevin. "Hey, don't use Stanton's government email," Kevin told me, "just use his personal email."

I had already sent the email to Stanton's city hall address, so the mayor had a staffer follow up with us to make it look official, just in case anyone came across our correspondence.

When Stanton found out our company would be making more than $1 million in profit off the Phoenix contract, he contacted Kevin about a campaign contribution. He assured Kevin that he would make sure that our company would get a contract before he resigned, if we could guarantee contributions to his congressional campaign.

Kevin called me after hearing this from Stanton, then asked me, "Are you good to direct some money to Stanton's campaign? If so, he will make sure that we get the contract before leaving office. But we need to guarantee it."

This was one of those turning points in my life. At this point, I was not yet working with the FBI. I thought it would be best to record this conversation with Kevin making the request for cash. I told him I had a call coming in and asked him if I could stop by his place later. I went home and gathered my recording device, and then I headed over to Kevin's. Little did I know, the FBI was already monitoring Kevin and his communications at this point.

When I got to Kevin's, he told me this was going to be a solid contract. That Greg Stanton was his boy and he would deliver. He told me that he told Stanton, "These guys are keyed up," referring to me, and that we could deliver if he did. He told me, "This dude needs money 'cause he's running." Meaning that Mayor Greg Stanton was now running for Congress and needed money for his campaign.

Kevin continued, "We've got to make him deliver something first. I can't give him too much."

We decided to give Stanton $15,000 in campaign contributions, with another $10,000 waiting in the wings after the contract was finalized. I told him that "we have a total of five maxes." A max referred to a maximum contribution to a campaign that someone could make. I personally supplied the $15,000 to Kevin.

Initially, the plan was to make contributions to Stanton's congressional campaign under various donor names, and the doors started to open for our contract to be put into place with the city.

Ultimately, I gave Kevin the $15,000 to take out to Stanton during one of his trips to Phoenix. Stanton set up the meetings and told the police department to get it done. It was clear that some people within the police department did not like the pressure they were getting from the mayor.

"We like figuring out who we are going to be working with and that's not something we like the mayor's office to tell us," one police leader told us. There was no opposition from members of the city council. However, thankfully, Kevin was friends with the chief of police.

Just as things were moving forward and looking good, Stanton decided to suddenly resign as mayor earlier than he told us to campaign full-time for Congress. We had not been expecting that.

"Don't worry," Stanton told us, "we'll get you a contract. And if not, if I get elected to Congress, I can still help you. I can change the federal laws on texting and driving, which will really help you. If I do not win, I will come back and finalize your contract, if it hasn't been done already."

When Stanton left the mayor's office, it did not take long for the contract to become dead in the water.

I remember being with Kevin at his business office in Oak Park, which was just a house, when Stanton reached out. He was asking about the remaining money for his campaign. Kevin showed me the text and I laughed. Little did I know that a few months down the road I would see this same text correspondence between Kevin and Stanton. However, it would not be either of them showing it to me. It would be the FBI.

Kevin figured he should call Stanton to see if it were possible to get the contract back on track, and that call became surprisingly interesting. Immediately after pleasantries, Stanton went straight into complaining about not getting enough press for his congressional campaign.

"What you need to do," Kevin told him, "is to create your own press."

"What do you mean?" Stanton asked.

"If there was an incident where you could be a hero or a survivor, that would be good," Kevin replied.

Then they started plotting a scheme for Stanton to get robbed outside a restaurant.

I was shocked yet entertained by all of this. Surely, they were only kidding? However, I knew better. Sure enough, within the next day or two, Stanton told police he had been robbed by a man with a weapon resembling a hatchet outside a restaurant in Phoenix.

The restaurant parking lot was full, so he parked on the street. After having dinner alone, he was heading back to his car when he was approached by a man who appeared to be homeless, Stanton told reporters.

"I assumed he was probably going through a difficult time—experiencing homelessness—and was going to ask for money," Stanton said. "I will often provide these people with resources."[1]

According to the news story, the man asked for money and Stanton offered to give him a few bucks to help, but the man forced him across the street into a darker area. Stanton told the man to take his wallet, then he ran back to the restaurant to call police, or so the story went. (Apparently no one questioned why he needed the restaurant phone to call the police—doesn't everyone have a cell phone these days?)

The fake robbery occurred late in the campaign, which Stanton won. At least I did not have to foot the bill for that stunt. I was out $15,000, but at least Stanton did not ask me to pay for the fake robbery. Greg Stanton is now a proud member of the US House of Representatives, faithfully making the laws of this nation.

In late 2019, when I was working for the FBI, Kevin set up an appointment with the new mayor of Phoenix, Kate Gallego. She seemed open to considering our company's services. In the meantime, things were heating up in New Haven and Los Angeles, so we never followed up with Mayor Gallego. There were too many city mayors Kevin had indicated had traded bribes for favors in the past, but there was not enough time to pursue all these leads.

CHAPTER SIX
A CHESS PLAYER

Throughout my time with Kevin, it became clear he was a chess player, using live humans as his pieces. Everything was business with him. There was a motive behind everything he did or said. At the end of the game, he had to be the one who walked away with the most.

Kevin thought that I was smart, and regarding certain things, I would say that I am. He often told me I reminded him of himself when he was my age. He would say that I had ambition and feared failure just as he did. This was also true. I forfeited a lot of the "fun with friends" in my twenties and early thirties to focus on business.

Nonetheless, with Kevin there was always an ask. He would pay me a compliment right before he was about to ask for something. When we would hang out, watching movies or television at his house, it was clear there was always an agenda. "We should talk about this; I've thought about this. I found this opportunity," he would say. It was never just relaxing and kicking up our feet.

His power became even more clear to me one day when he summoned me to his house the week of my birthday. It was in March 2016, and I was having a busy week. Kevin had gotten me connected with the NBA leadership, and my company, Quicklegal, had been selected as one of the finalists in the NBA Sacramento Kings Capitalize competition event. We would later go on to win, taking first place. I was also in Silicon Valley at the Facebook headquarters, meeting with executives and partaking in a Facebook event. Times were busy. However, when Kevin requested me, I went.

He lived in Sacramento's Fabulous Forties neighborhood. The Fab Forties neighborhood is part of the East Sacramento district. Former President Ronald Reagan lived there while serving most of his term as governor of California. The Fab Forties is known as the elite neighborhood where all the millionaires reside.

Kevin was having a bad day because a journalist was writing a negative article about sexual allegations against him from his days as a player for the Phoenix Suns to his most current affair. The current allegations came from a minor named Mandi Koba. She accused him of molesting her when she was 15. A 2016 documentary detailed allegations from this woman and four others stating they were victims.

"They all wanted me, my fame, and money," Kevin told me. "You know how it is, right? They see us, see how we are coming up, and they want some of it. They know that they can't get it for free. We ain't marrying these bitches. Then they act all surprised when it is pay-up time. You know what I'm talking about."

I did not have a clue what he meant. The relationships that I had in no way compared to anything he was referencing. However, I started to see that he thought he was "the man" and "invincible." He believed he could do whatever he wanted to do.

There was reportedly a settlement between Mandi Koba and Kevin for more than $233,000, in which she agreed never to speak about Johnson to anyone other than "a priest, a therapist, or a lawyer."[1] However, given this crazy resolution, it would not be the last of such events. Similar allegations continued popping up wherever Kevin went, including Sacramento City Hall. I could see it when I was with him. Kevin seemed to be undressing employees with his eyes.

Kevin told me that when the cases were being investigated in Phoenix, he had hired an opposition firm to dig up dirt on the police investigators and potential prosecutors. That is how he got advance notice when Mandi Koba (the first victim, a minor at the time of the incident) showed up at the Phoenix Police Department to make a pretext call to Kevin to try to catch him talking about their sexual relations. A law enforcement official from inside the department reached out to Kevin, tipping him off to her presence there. Kevin's source told him the detective and Mandi Koba were about to call him to get him on a recorded line to try to incriminate himself. He answered the call but, having been tipped off, denied any sexual contact with her.

I was shocked when he told me that story. I was even more shocked he was tied in with the Phoenix Police Department. He was able to jump on a phone call with the chief of police and get whatever he needed. This was brought to light when he reached out to the chief to assist him in with the mayor's office to get a contract in the city. It was like everyone knew that they had to get on board with him or face his wrath. Most joined him. Kevin was good at taking care of his people. He would find something that they needed or wanted and then make sure he got it to them, if they played along and did what he demanded.

"It's just a game," he said. "You just have to move the pieces and think a couple of steps ahead of them."

I remember driving home that night thinking this was crazy. It was like what I had seen in the movies. The "bad guys" were the people in power. They were the ones with the money and the glamour. They controlled some of the police, the judges, had connections everywhere, and were even friends with the President of the United States.

In late 2017, Kevin and I started making trips to New York, Phoenix, and all over the country for several years during our relationship. It was for business. Kevin and I would meet with mayors, celebrities, NBA officials, businesspeople, and private investigators.

One of our trips was to the East Coast, where Kevin was to meet with SeedInvest, which was the biggest online crowd-sourced investing platform. Kevin wanted to set up a fund that focused on raising capital from minorities to help fund black-owned businesses. Now this was something that I could get behind. However, it was not long until Kevin figured out a plan. He would get an advance kickback from the companies that were to receive investments.

Kevin's power really transformed in 2014 when he was "elected" President of the United States Conference of Mayors. He told me it was one of his best moves ever. He set up backdoor agreements, payments, and favors to win that position. It was the most powerful position he held.

The US Conference of Mayors would hold meetings with high-profile individuals, such as Barack Obama, Hillary Clinton, Nancy Pelosi, and the Dalai Lama. It also connected with big companies. This group had access to, and, more importantly, influence from, the top of the political heap on down. If mayors needed help in their cities, Kevin could get the right people on board to do whatever needed to be done. If mayors found themselves in trouble within their own cities, Kevin could help. Sometimes, the mayors did not know the cause of their troubles was the man who they were going to for help.

Mayors began doing Kevin favors to get his backing for their program and initiatives. He leveraged these relationships perfectly. The incredible thing was how other mayors, senators, and members of Congress were on board with this. As Kevin said, it was all a big chess game—a game in which I knew Kevin would soon expose all the pieces in federal court to help save himself and reduce his sentence.

Not everything was easy, though. Some mayors, like Eric Garcetti of Los Angeles and Bill de Blasio of New York, were harder for Kevin to influence. This was because they had national political status. Some would say they had as much power as the president.

However, there was a time when Mayor Garcetti needed Kevin.

CHAPTER SEVEN
CONFIDENTIAL HUMAN SOURCE

A week after my meeting with the US Attorney's Office and several law enforcement departments under the Department of Justice, the AUSA reached out to my attorney. They needed to have one more meeting, get me to sign a proffer and cooperation agreement, and ask me a few more questions. These are agreements the government and the defendants enter into stating the government will not prosecute them for the crimes for which they have been charged. The exception is murder and a few other serious crimes. In return, the defendants work with the government to solve cases and help give back to the communities that, at one point, had been damaged by the criminals and their actions.

How these related to my case was dependent on how much I helped the FBI and the US Attorney's Office, and that would determine how much they helped me with my case. Awkwardly enough, it was a legal quid pro quo arrangement. Their goal was to catch Kevin. If I helped them, then they would help me put my case behind me once and for all. Or so I thought.

When I arrived to meet with the AUSA Todd Pickles and FBI, I assumed this would be another long meeting. However, it was not.

There were only a few people in attendance. There were two AUSAs, two FBI agents, and my case officer (the woman who arrested me and oversaw the investigation in my case). We did the formalities, went over the proffer, and a cooperation agreement. They explained the differences and asked me if I had any questions. I did not. Once we signed the paperwork, I noticed a quickened pace in our conversation.

"Mr. Bluford, to prepare for our meeting, I want you to think about dates, transactions, events, and people. Make a list of things that we should look into and verify," said one of the FBI agents.

"That will be easy," I said.

"What do you mean?" asked the FBI agent.

"I have been collecting recordings, emails, texts, and conversations of Kevin, other mayors, and corrupt people who Kevin introduced me to since the beginning," I replied.

I remember the shocked looked on their faces, them looking at one another, and then quickly trying to remove the looks of shock from their faces.

"You do?" asked one of the agents.

"Yes. Of course. If Kevin were to ever get caught for any of the things he had me involved in, he would surely throw me under the bus. I wanted to make sure to capture audio and video of him, so that if things ever came to light, people would see who was in charge and who did exactly what," I explained.

I knew it was smart to record any illegal activity. As I mentioned, there were just too many occasions in my life when I got in trouble because I was the poor black kid with a past, and the other person was white or a person with influence. I told myself, regardless of it being illegal, I would not allow myself to be put in that position again.

"Well, that's great," said the agent.

They asked me to bring everything I had to the next meeting and to not make copies of anything. They wanted all my original files. The FBI agents told me they would be in contact shortly to schedule my visit to the office.

As the next few days passed, I remembered coming down with the flu. As always, it was horrible, and I was on bedrest trying to get better.

I still remember getting the text message from Special Agent Reggie Coleman of the FBI. While at home in bed, a random phone number called me. I did not answer it because I did not know the number. Then a text came. *Mr. Bluford. This is Special Agent Reggie Coleman with the FBI. I hope you feel better soon. Are you able to meet with us next Thursday?* I was shocked. How did he know I was sick? Nonetheless, I did not ask any questions and promptly agreed to meet with them.

Driving to the FBI office that early morning in March had me once again thinking about life. I was already several weeks into the MRT program, and it was starting to change the way I saw things. I wanted to make sure I was motivated to do the right thing because it was the right thing to do, and not simply because it was going to help me.

I thought about it and asked myself why I was doing this. Then I remembered. I had been informed that Kevin was possibly involved in sex trafficking of minors. No child should ever have to face this. Having been a victim of child molestation myself, I knew that if I could do something to help kids, then, without question, I would commit and do it.

I arrived early at the Roseville office. There was no way anyone could ever get into this building uninvited. The exterior security was first class. Armed private security and patrols were everywhere. I checked in and gave them my identification. They searched me thoroughly. Initially, there was a small issue because I had brought my cell phone inside. No cell phones were allowed in the FBI from non-employees. However, I told them I had evidence on it that the agents had requested that I bring.

After about 15 minutes, FBI agent Reggie Coleman came and got me. He walked me around the building and gave me a little information about the FBI and this building. It looked and seemed really cool. This was the FBI. He could tell I was enjoying this. I was smiling and looking around as if I were a kid in a candy store. As we approached the main building, Special Agent Reggie Coleman said, "Mr. Bluford, you are now entering one of the most secure buildings on the West Coast."

Thankfully, before this meeting, I had done my best to prepare for it. I was not certain if this was going to be a friendly meeting or more of an interview and interrogation. Nonetheless, I had prepared for all scenarios. I contacted some of my own federal law enforcement resources to ask general questions about how these meetings go. I was hoping it would be an informal, conversational meeting where we would review the recordings.

We went into a conference room. Special Agent Rebekah Bills and others were there. She had been with the FBI for quite some time and was known publicly for taking down many sex trafficking organizations and people.[1] The agents quickly introduced themselves, and then we jumped into business.

"Did you bring the recordings with you?" asked Special Agent Coleman.

"Yes," I said.

I took out my flash drive device and printed material. They already had a laptop set up and ready to go. We sat there and reviewed some of the items.

Special Agent Coleman said, "Well, this is okay evidence, but I could argue it the other way. We really don't have anything here." I could immediately tell that Special Agent Bills and the other agents in the room did not concur. I knew I was being bluffed because of the facial reactions the other agents wore when Special Agent Coleman made his comment, and during some of the recordings where I had captured clear quid pro quos.

However, Special Agent Coleman was taking the approach of making me feel like I did not have anything of value to offer him, and that I would therefore have to prove my value. I believe he assessed me from my file and realized when walking me around the FBI compound that I was impressed and liked this type of life. He decided to go the route of trying to manipulate me to think I had to prove myself to him. That did not go so well.

I had been previously briefed on this process. Instead of playing the whole good agent, bad agent game, I said, "Be quiet, I'm going to make a call." At this point, I took out my cell phone to call Kevin Johnson.

I called Kevin on the speakerphone and said, "Hey, how's it going?"

He answered, "Hey, what's up?"

"I am going to Phoenix and there is another RFP opportunity there," I told him. Previously, Mayor Greg Stanton had not delivered on the first RFP. I continued, "I'm thinking he might be able to push another one our way."

Kevin said, "Absolutely. We gave that guy $15,000 and then he decided to resign early as mayor and run for Congress. Do you want me to connect you?"

The agents smiled in disbelief.

Yet, once I got off the phone, Special Agent Coleman still tried to play it off. He said, "Okay. Still, how do we know this is Kevin Johnson on the tapes?"

I was thinking, *Okay, tough guy,* but I just said, "I also have video to share." I did not like the way this meeting was going. If this thing was going to move forward, I would have to be sure to track everything so that no one tried to throw me under the bus if things did not work out. This guy was challenging me left and right, and it was all for show. *Why?* I was thinking.

I left the FBI office thinking, *This is not going to work. I do not want to work with such an agent.* I went home, discussed it with my attorney, and made other plans. At the end of the day, I was not afraid to face the consequences of my actions. In fact, I welcomed it. It was a means to get everything over with. This request was from the government. I did not need help nor request it. I could walk away and be fine moving forward with my own case.

My attorney received a call from the US Attorney's Office shortly after my meeting at the FBI office. He was told that the FBI wanted to move forward with my cooperation, and in return would offer me a 5K1 letter. This serves as a higher cooperation document which goes directly to the judge in a case. It tells the judge that the person assisted the government in various ways against other criminals and requests that the judge sentence the individual outside the federal sentencing guidelines.

My attorney informed them I was open to helping them, however, he told them I did not want to work with the leading agent anymore. If they wanted me, they needed to have someone else in charge. Not even a day later, the FBI contacted my attorney and informed him that Special Agent Reggie Coleman was no longer working this case.

The new case agent for this investigation was Special Agent Rebekah Bills. I had remembered meeting her at the FBI office. She seemed nice, quiet, and smart. Once I started working with her, I had to admit she probably had the best memory I have ever seen in my life. However, do not be fooled, she had the ability to flip a switch and turn into an ass-kicker really damn quick.

Until the end, we mostly had a decent working relationship. Some of the other agents who I worked with were Special Agent Rachael La'Chappelle, Special Agent Austin Harper, and Special Agent Russ. It is important to mention that my undercover name at this point was "The Lobbyist." It would be my code name used outside of my confidential human source number. This would be the name used in all court documents, warrants, and subpoenas.

It did not take long for the FBI to recognize my hard work and success rate. As I began working more with the agents, we started to develop a better professional relationship. Early on in our relationship, I was going to the FBI office and working with the agents. Sometimes, I would set up shop and work with them in their offices, and other times I would just go and dump my phone, which meant download everything on it to a backup database. Other times, I would just need to go in to get a new recording device, which was FBI-issued, and give them my used devices.

At some point, a few people started getting suspicious about me and my case. The FBI decided to have me not come to the office any longer. I started meeting my team, and sometimes new agents, at undisclosed locations, and sometimes in public. I would occasionally meet with Special Agent Bills and Special Agent La'Chappelle at Starbucks. I remember how I would just stop and smile. Little did the people around us know what we were doing and how our work would affect their entire city, let alone the nation. Yet, here we were in Starbucks with our Grande white mochas and cappuccinos, just hanging out.

I seemed to have a talent for law enforcement. The agents I worked with were often surprised by my quick success in the goals we set in the case. From the beginning, I was able to help them connect some dots regarding corruption at Sacramento City Hall regarding some of the RAILS grants and the main players involved.

However, there would be points where I would make mistakes. I cannot mention these at this time, as I am sure the criminal defense attorneys who will be representing these individuals would love to use them to defend and get these people off. Nonetheless, for the first time in a long time, I finally felt at home . . . and in my element. I felt like this new profession could become my lifelong work.

The agents proposed making this a long-term arrangement, like in the famous case of con artist Frank Abagnale Jr. Most people will recognize the name from the 2002 hit move *Catch Me If You Can*, in which Leonardo DiCaprio played Abagnale. Frank was a mastermind manipulator and fraudster, but he turned into the FBI's most valuable confidential human source. Frank went on to help the FBI solve, catch, and close hundreds of cases. He still works for the FBI as an independent contractor and a confidential human source.

CHAPTER EIGHT
FAVORS

For this investigation to work, the FBI had to make sure we could track and prove that Kevin was doing the things he was doing for his own benefit.

Government App Solutions, formerly Text To Ticket, was initially launched around 2016 to help fight distracted driving. As mentioned earlier, the owners and I created a mobile app where the general public could capture people who were texting and driving, submit the violation, and then have the driver or registered owner of the vehicle receive a ticket in the mail.

The way it worked was if a pedestrian or a passenger in a car saw a person driving a vehicle and using a mobile device, the user would launch our app on their phone. All they would need to do was press the record button and capture the vehicle, vehicle license plate, and a clear video of the driver using their mobile device. That was it. The user could submit the video and get paid $5.

On the technical side of the app, it would track the user's location, time, and date, encrypt the video frames, and digitalize them to ensure the evidence was original and not tampered with. It was almost the exact same process red-light traffic cameras had implemented. From there, all submissions would be forwarded to us, then we would vet the videos and then forward them to local law enforcement. It was quite an innovative solution for addressing such a rapidly growing problem.

The company had great traction early on. Two months after launch, the company applied to get into an incubator and accelerator program called 500 Startups, founded by Dave McClure, a wealthy investor with a history of success from his PayPal, Microsoft, and Facebook days. It was known throughout the tech world to be one of the best, if not *the* best, incubators and accelerators around. It was the elite venture capital firm for startups and gave them invaluable training and access to the rest of Silicon Valley in exchange for equity in their startups. It also came with a $150,000 check. The company received thousands of applications and generally only accepted 30 to 40.

Kevin Johnson was friends with the main partner, Dave McClure, and I was no stranger to this organization. I had previously been accepted into this program a few years back when I had my old company, Quicklegal. Though I never got close to Dave McClure, he and Kevin had hit it off. They were working on a deal to bring a branch of 500 Startups to Sacramento, California. However, that plan would not make it off the ground. Dave McClure resigned due to sexual harassment claims and other allegations.

As the company started to grow, we were having trouble picking up contracts with the government. No one was a fan of texting and driving citations, and that was because most Americans were guilty of it. Also, it was not a smart political move for elected officials. The people who would be receiving tickets were the people who would be voting in the next term. So, we had to expand our services and produce other ways to use our technology to help the government solve problems.

After several weeks, we decided to use the same technology and tailor it to the parking enforcement and code enforcement division. Users, community members, or parking enforcement officers could use the app, capture the violation, and submit it. From there, the registered owner would receive the parking citation in the mail, or the city could elect to use mobile printers to print the citations in real time and place them on the vehicle's windshield.

Now it was time to get out there and start pitching our product to local governments. This was a long, expensive, and burdensome process. However, it was honest. Yet, this was not pleasing to Kevin, and therefore he came up with his own plan. He knew the mayors and knew what they wanted. He would buy and bully his way to success, as that had always worked for him in the past.

I remember at times during the FBI investigation being amazed at how easily these mayors would set up fake meetings with all the right people, and then send us the contract through a sole/single source agreement, or they would put out an RFP and select us as the winner after the "due diligence" process. The funny thing was that often, our company did not meet the requirements of the local governments. Not because we did not have a sound company or product, but they often required five years of experience, other government contracts for reference, and certain other requirements.

During the investigation, Kevin shot himself in the foot by giving me a list of mayors and other politicians who owed him favors. This included those who had taken bribes from him, requested bribes, and, most importantly, who had campaigns coming up that we could "help out" in exchange for them giving our company a contract with their cities.

And by "help out," I mean give them cash under the table in return for their guarantee of influence in getting our private company lucrative contracts with their cities, or to a company Kevin owned that would be willing to pay him for it. I had to turn that list of mayors, members of Congress, and others over to the FBI and the US Attorney's Office. It did not take long for them to come back. It was almost as if they now had an à la carte menu. They came back and said, "We want these people right here." This would be the first phase of investigations. I noticed that everyone selected was a Democrat. *Interesting*, I noted.

Thanks to Kevin and his list of corrupt politicians, getting to these people was no longer a problem. Now I did not even have to email cities or make calls. The mayors and their chiefs of staff were calling Kevin and me to set up meetings. It was crazy. The FBI wanted to make sure we were capturing all of this.

At this point, what the agents were asking of me was way over the amount of time and the number of people of interest they had originally asked me to help them gather information on. It was not what we had agreed to back when I had entered into my proffer and cooperation agreement. However, again, I knew that I was doing the right thing, and that I would be finally giving back to the community and repaying my debt to society. More importantly, after having seen the evidence they had against Kevin for other sexual crimes, and having been a victim when I was a child, I was now personally committed to taking him down.

From the beginning, in early 2018, when it was decided we would use Government App Solutions as the front company, it was always challenging for the Department of Justice to move forward at certain times in the case because it did not want to interfere and hurt a business that had no idea what Kevin Johnson or these corrupt mayors and other politicians were doing. Neither did I. After all, these were my friends who owned and ran the company.

The Department of Justice decided to take on a lot of the burden. The FBI provided me with lots of cash to cover expenses for the business, such as for development of technology (meetings, meals, travel, and lodging) that was specific for the cities we were going after as part of our investigation. However, there was a time when the company believed it was doing better based on the contracts it was getting, so they, in turn, took on new risk and opportunities based on false information and data that was being supplied by the FBI through me. This created some exposure and liability for the government.

However, because Kevin Johnson was a shareholder of the front company, both the FBI and the US Attorney's Office agreed to play it step-by-step until everyone could figure out a way to separate the innocent company from what Kevin was doing.

At one point, the FBI and the US Attorney's Office decided that they would outright acquire Government App Solutions. It was too much liability, and, at the end, all the FBI actions would surely destroy the company that was being used without its permission as a front. After all, this company had a valuation of about $12 million, and that is a big liability and gamble to take.

We devised a plan to buy the company around October 2018. The US Department of Justice has access to plenty of what are called shell companies which it sets up. It creates tax returns, fake owners, and aliases to run these companies. When they are just air companies, an agent can get an identification card that matches the CEO's name, or, in some cases, me or another confidential human source. For this, though, we went with a company that wanted to outright buy the company and its technology. The pitch was going to be that I knew the CEO, and I would handhold the deal and make sure it got done.

However, the CEO was not an undercover agent. The FBI introduced a new player into the game. He was a civilian as I was, and a confidential human source and independent contractor for the FBI. He was already known in the Sacramento area as a business guy, so the FBI thought that would be best as Kevin could vet him with his local resources.

As the negotiations began, the FBI was getting a lot of pressure for wanting to spend such a large amount of money for the Kevin Johnson case. On top of that, the company was not really being flexible when it came to its valuation and selling amount. I took a personal loss of several hundred thousand dollars trying to get the company to play ball. However, the acquisition eventually stopped.

The idea was for the FBI to try to license the technology of the company and open its own government technology company. The company would give me fake equity and give Kevin equity, based on services and his return to the company. Again, the government was sensitive to avoid potentially hurting any innocent parties in the front company. However, due to resistance from the higher levels of FBI bureaucracy, we decided to not run with it. It was too expensive to license and run the technology with FBI employees, and we were running out of time. Washington wanted to take down the case.

One of the unfortunate factors of this FBI investigation and sting is that Government App Solutions was being used without its knowledge or consent. Because Kevin Johnson was a shareholder of the company and was illegally directing contracts there, the company would surely take a financial hit or be forced to close. However, not all would be lost for Government App Solutions—there are certain legal recourses available to a company in this situation, to help keep it alive and thriving.

CHAPTER NINE
LOS ANGELES

The owner of the Los Angeles Clippers, billionaire Donald Sterling, was taped in April 2014 making racist comments to his mistress. Sterling had been triggered by his mistress posting pictures of herself with Magic Johnson on Instagram.

"It bothers me a lot that you want to broadcast that you're associating with black people," Sterling could be heard saying on the tape. "You can sleep with [black people]. You can bring them in, you can do whatever you want" but "the little I ask you is . . . not to bring them to my games."[1]

It was a public relations disaster for Los Angeles and the NBA. Kevin became an advisor on this issue to the NBA Players' Union. He urged Adam Silver, the NBA commissioner, to impose a stiff penalty on Sterling. Silver did just that, banning Sterling from the NBA for life. Sterling sold the team.

Kevin was at the top of his game in 2014, and Mayor Eric Garcetti called on him for help. The people of Los Angeles were infuriated and demanding action from the NBA and Mayor Garcetti because the team was there. The City of Los Angeles was protesting. Activists, civil rights groups, and celebrities were demanding action. A city riot was destined. However, when Mayor Kevin Johnson stepped in, he did what he always did best. He called all the right people and put on a display show for the people.

He appeared at a news conference with Garcetti and basketball great Kareem Abdul-Jabbar. He told the *Sacramento Bee* that his work on the Sterling case "feels like the most important thing I've done since I've been mayor."[2]

The city was saved. The crisis was thankfully averted, and the people of LA seemed to be at peace with the resolution that had been promised, and at peace that Kevin Johnson, a black man, was in charge. Garcetti now owed Kevin.

It just so happened that Kevin would want to call on Mayor Garcetti to help our company, Government App Solutions, get a contract with the City of Los Angeles.

A parking enforcement contract with Los Angeles would have been the crown jewel, making us all richer overnight. There would have been as much as $150 million in annual revenue. Our company would have received 10 to 20 percent of that per year. With the Los Angeles contract, the company would easily have been valued at $100 million and would have been acquired by another company in no time. Kevin, who already had an estimated net worth of between $10 and $15 million, would go from rich to super-rich.

Kevin said it was time to have Garcetti come through and repay the favor. It was not long before Kevin reached out and negotiated an agreement with Mayor Garcetti to get the City of Los Angeles, specifically the Los Angeles Department of Transportation (LADOT), a $150 million parking enforcement contract with the city. This was not a bad deal in return for only one favor.

The FBI had access to emails, text messages, and recorded calls. However, things would sometimes get tricky when certain city staff would have internal meetings regarding pushing Government App Solutions along. They needed to get Mayor Garcetti, Kevin Johnson, and internal city staff on record pushing the company through, and their opportunity came. The mayor was having Borja Leon, who at the time was the deputy mayor of transportation, push the folks at LADOT to get things done. However, when LADOT would push back, the mayor himself would reach out. This was gold. This was what the FBI needed.

Kevin set it up so he and Garcetti would divide 15 percent in kickbacks among themselves. Kevin was crazy enough to put this in the form of a written contract with his attorney and the company Government App Solutions. He presented the deal to the company as: if he was able to work hard and get the company a major contract with the City of Los Angeles, then he would also want a revenue share from it. The fact was, Kevin never really shared information about the company to Mayor Garcetti to get the contract.

Once the company agreed, Garcetti started to perform immediately. It was a quick handoff before we met with LADOT. We were assured that everything would go smoothly. Garcetti told us, "Everything is already set up. We'll push it from here. If things slow down, just reach out to Kevin, and Kevin will reach out to me, and we'll get it going."

However, Garcetti knew that he would need to get a few city council members on board to approve this contract once the RFP went out. Kevin told us that Garcetti had a few council members who would automatically vote his way, however, we should meet with council member José Huizar and make sure he was "taken care of" so we got his vote, also.

It was unheard of and unorthodox for Garcetti to be meeting and pushing an individual company on a contract of this size. The normal procedure would have been for the city to put out an RFP so that all companies could have an equal shot at getting the contract. All proposals would be reviewed and considered equally and impartially. But this was not legitimate. This was dirty politics. This multimillion-dollar contract was being walked by hand and forced through Los Angeles City Hall personally by the mayor.

I was driving to LADOT to meet with the executive management team and others from the parking enforcement department. Any time people did not go along with the program, Kevin would reach out to Garcetti and get them back on board. This is when Garcetti had the director of transportation reach out to LADOT to address the frustrations Garcetti was having with the department. It was clear from emails I was receiving from LADOT and the communication LADOT was getting from Garcetti that Garcetti was directing the things that were to get done. I remember the chief of parking enforcement becoming nonresponsive at one point. He was, in fact, favoring one of the other larger companies that had already been providing services to the city. I told Kevin about this, and he immediately reached out to Garcetti.

I remember the next day, on May 25, 2018, the chief of parking enforcement emailed me, writing, "I received direction from the mayor's office and he would like us to explore opportunities in deploying your application." And just like that, I once again saw the power of Kevin and bought-and-paid-for politicians. They do not let anyone get in the way of their money. A company trying to conduct business on the up-and-up would never have been able to get a phone call from the executives at LADOT or the mayor, much less a face-to-face meeting. But money buys access.

Sometimes though, even I would get straightened out. It was clear from meetings and phone calls that Garcetti and Kevin were running the show; however, we were not ever to put any of that in writing. I once mistakenly sent an email to LADOT executive management regarding Garcetti's position, and the chief wrote back that he had heard from Garcetti's office to explore options. I then got a call from Garcetti's office informing me to be careful about the emails and not to put anything in writing. Simultaneously, I also received a call from Kevin telling me the same thing, and adding "not to be stupid." He said that emails sent to public employees' work emails could be requested by the public, and told me not to email them at their work accounts.

I remember the chief of parking enforcement asking me to coffee one day. He was one of the highest-ranking staff there. He asked me,

"What's going on with your company and the mayor's office?" I knew I could not tell him. He seemed to be genuinely concerned, and I think he was on to us. I reported this to Kevin and Garcetti. The next week, I received a random email from that same staff member saying he knew it was short notice, but he was retiring immediately. I believe he was an ethical guy and was forced out because he challenged the mayor on this contract.

Our negotiations continued after he left. By this time, Garcetti had already had us and LADOT work out a letter of intent and a memorandum of understanding in advance. This was a strict no-no. The city was not legally allowed to enter into these types of agreements because these contracts were supposed to be up for fair bidding. Everyone and every business were supposed to have a "fair" chance to bid on contracts. However, like most corrupt deals, they would never even have any chance at all. The game was rigged.

Then the general manager of LADOT got wind of things. She objected to the heavy-handed involvement by Garcetti's office with this contract. She worked to put a stop to it. I remember her stating in one email, "No. I want to talk to staff, not elected officials." I knew she would give us a run for our money; however, in the end, like most people, she did not want to lose her job by not playing ball.

As the months began to pass and progress was advancing toward the contract, more people started getting curious about what was going on. The civil servants inside the Los Angeles government started getting upset. They began to push back. There were delays. I would reach out to Kevin, and Kevin would contact Garcetti. But then nothing moved forward. What was going on?

Then Kevin FaceTimed me one night, which was odd because he had never done that before.

"Hey, D. How's it going? Do you have minute?" he asked.

"Yeah. What's going on?" I said.

"We gotta push the brakes on LA a little," he said hesitantly.

"Why?" I said trying to catch my breath.

"Remember the city council member you met with, José Huizar?

He just got raided by the FBI. Do not worry; we are good. However, Garcetti wants to take it slow for now. See how things play out. He has someone at the FBI who's keeping him up to date, but for now there is no need to take any risk," he said.[3]

"Yeah. Okay."

CHAPTER TEN
CORRUPTION EVERYWHERE

P olitical corruption had become a major focus of crime for the FBI. In 2008, the FBI created the International Corruption Unit to oversee the increasing number of investigations involving global fraud against the US government and the corruption of federal public officials outside the continental US involving US funds, people, 6reand businesses. To put it in simple terms, the FBI wanted to start cracking down on corrupt elected officials taking money and bribes in exchange for contracts within their cities.

Public corruption, the FBI's top criminal investigative priority, poses a fundamental threat to our national security and way of life. It can affect everything from how well our borders are secured and our neighborhoods protected to how verdicts are handed down in courts to how public infrastructure such as roads and schools are built. It also takes a significant toll on the public's pocketbooks by siphoning off tax dollars—it is estimated that public corruption costs the U.S. government and the public billions of dollars each year. The FBI is uniquely situated to combat corruption, with the skills and capabilities to run complex undercover operations and surveillance.[1]

A quick online search would shock readers to learn how much political corruption is going on. Many mayors are getting indicted. Catherine Pugh (former mayor of Baltimore, Maryland) was indicted in 2019 on fraud charges over her book scam. Dennis Tyler (former mayor of Muncie, Indiana) was indicted in 2019 for accepting bribes in exchange for contracts. Rick Sollars (mayor of Taylor, Michigan) was indicted in 2019, along with two others, for using the power of his political seat to gain money personally. And that is not even half of them.

Again, it goes to show what is really happening in American politics. People ask, "What is happening in my city hall?" These mayors picked one crime they felt comfortable with and ran with it. If it was extorting businesses in exchange for quicker permits, they did that. If it was accepting bribes for contracts, they did that.

However, Kevin Johnson mastered them all. He could pull strings and make everything work. He was so powerful in his group of mayors that he would say, "Jump," and they would ask, "How high?" Many would say this is too much power for one man. Yet, there he was. Collectively, hundreds of millions of dollars of contracts were being stolen from the American people and being kept and given through back-door deals to and by politicians and the highest bidders. How can this change?

The real question is this. What is there to do when corrupt politicians also have the law enforcement, prosecutors, and judges on their side? Remember, Kevin Johnson had been notified by a law enforcement official in Phoenix they were going to try to capture him on a pretext call with the minor Mandi Koba, who he had sexual relations with. Then, he was tipped off regarding the federal government pursuing him.

Kevin began his search for dirt on those pursuing him, and he found it—and ultimately turned away everyone who was trying to catch him. And if he could not find anything, he would create something. Kevin believed that married men were generally the easiest to go after. If someone was giving him trouble, or not going along, he would spend money to learn about these individuals through opposition firms.

An opposition firm is a group of highly skilled people who collect and analyze information about a specific individual. They are mainly used in campaigns. Opposition research can take many different forms. Generally, and most commonly, opposition research is based on a candidate's past policy missteps. However, at other times, it can be made up of personal indiscretions. What all opposition research has in common is that it is information specifically obtained to enhance the understanding of the target's weaknesses. For Kevin, this was always ideal.

Kevin would always find people in power, especially during his years sitting as mayor, who wanted to challenge him. It would be a game they would lose. Kevin would hire the best people for opposition research and find out this person's moves and events scheduled for the next month. He would then coordinate with as associate who owned an escort company to set the bait.

He always believed that if you gave a married man a few drinks and put a pretty woman in front of him, he would forget his wedding vows. And sadly enough, he was always correct. Kevin would always instruct the escorts to set up a few hidden cameras in the room, which is where they always took the target.

Then, when Kevin would get the video footage, he would always send a one-time random letter with a copy of the material to his target, with clear instructions to either stop opposing or challenging something specific or to vote for this or that.

I remember sometimes being in on these meetings, thinking, *No way this is going to work.* However, then he would pull it off. Kevin would always ask, "Do you know what the 'm' in mayor stands for? Mighty. The mighty always win."

CHAPTER ELEVEN
TAKING DOWN A MONSTER

In the months leading up to the FBI raid of council member José Huizar, Kevin had been getting suspicious about his inner circle, which was not comprised of many people. In particular, Kevin and his wife Michelle were growing suspicious and frustrated with Kevin's longtime friend, Tracy Stigler. Tracy had been one of Kevin's most trusted friends, even uprooting his life and moving to Sacramento from Phoenix. This move would cost him his law license, as it was alleged he did not inform his clients about it. He just picked up and left at the direction of Kevin.

Throughout the years, Tracy would serve as an advocate for Kevin, trying his best to shield him from liabilities, burying his mistakes, and helping bring down those who tried to challenge him. Text messages revealed through a public records request showed that Tracy had been caught red-handed setting up people to spy on the mayor's opponents when the National Conference of Black Mayors sued Kevin. It was ironic. Kevin had always preached to the general public that he stands for blacks trying to better themselves. However, here he was trying to destroy all the black mayors who had united to go against him.[1]

Nonetheless, Michelle was growing frustrated with Tracy missing deadlines and not being able to serve her and her husband to their standards anymore. During this time, they were trying to open a restaurant, get the Black Capital business going, and venture off into several other endeavors. Yet, things were not falling into place as planned. It seemed like Tracy had lost his way and did not have what it took any longer to get things done, whether it was the right way or under the table.

The time came for Kevin and Michelle to get rid of Tracy. However, they knew they would have to do it in the right way. After all, Tracy was a man who knew many secrets. Secrets that could destroy them. The FBI saw this as an opportunity, and I was to use this opportunity to expedite my relationship with Tracy and grow closer to find out what I could.

As Tracy and I started to spend more time together, Kevin got word and soon grew suspicious of me. He had received a text message from one of his staff who saw Tracy and I at lunch. Kevin then sent me a text message asking if I was free to meet up later. Thankfully, we (the FBI) had live access to all his texts and the agent in charge notified me. We decided to have me reply, "Yes. Funny thing is I was just going to message you. Need to give you the heads-up about something." This would set the tone and allow me to come to the meeting telling Kevin that Tracy was out to take him down. This, we believed, should encourage Kevin regarding our relationship and remove any doubts that he may have been having about me.

I went to meet with Kevin shortly after.

"Hey, D, you good?" he said.

"Ehh. Not really."

"What's going on," he said.

"Well, this morning I got a text from Tracy. He asked me to meet up because it was important. So, I did. This guy is trying to take you down," I said.

I could see that the energy from Kevin's body had immediately left. Just the idea made him sick. I could see the hairs raised on his arms. However, he tried to act confident.

"What do you mean? What did he say?" Kevin asked.

"Well, he was just telling me to be careful, because you are doing some illegal lobbying in Hawaii, then he was talking about the AmeriCorps investigation, and how you and others buried it, and that now he was working to help uncover it," I said.

None of this was true, however, the FBI agents had these as points of interest that they needed more information about. They believed that by having me say this, it would trigger Kevin to reach out to people and make sure they all started covering their asses. And it worked.

"Nah. He's just mad because we had to let him go. He wasn't performing. But look, I gotta run. Something came up right before you got here," he said.

"Yeah. No worries. Hit me later and let me know if you need me to do anything. I can play along with this to find out more information if you want," I told him.

"Yeah. I'll keep you posted," he replied.

This, in turn, led to a few things happening. Kevin did start reaching out to people to give them an update and let them know Tracy was working with someone/an organization to uncover their crimes and corruption. However, in turn, they all came to the conclusion that they needed to flush out everyone who was in their close circles to make sure they were still solid and loyal. This included me.

Kevin would then turn to the opposition research firm to investigate those closest to him. The questions started to be asked. "What is Derek Bluford doing with most of his time? Why is his case still open?" These were big red flags, and problems we had to solve immediately.

The FBI thought it would be best for me to go out and get a regular job for public display. However, the challenge with this was that I was still personally under indictment. In addition, I had not been an employee in almost a decade. I had owned most of the companies I had worked for. However, because one of my companies was a coworking space, I decided to look for open positions in that industry.

Within a few weeks, I applied and was hired as a community manager at a coworking company called WeWork. It was a challenging experience. I was in charge of the Berkeley, California location, which meant I had a four-hour commute total, there and back. I would generally have to get up about 5 a.m. to drive the two hours to work and get everything ready to open. Then I would close and head home after 6 p.m. And I did not get to just drive home. I would generally have to then drive to the FBI office to meet my team and work some more. It was such a challenging time.

However, there were some great things that I got from WeWork. I met some amazing colleagues and customers. A friend of mine, Nick, was in charge of sales. One day, he shared with me that he was writing a book. I was fascinated by his idea and what he was doing. I remember driving home thinking about it, and then playing with the idea of myself writing a book regarding everything I was currently working on.

That evening, I bounced the idea off my boss at the FBI. I asked her if it would be okay if I wrote a book regarding everything I was doing on this case. She granted me permission to write the book, but stated I could not share or publish it until everything went public.

Throughout the several months of working at WeWork, calls would sometimes pop up with corrupt public officials which I would have to take. I remember when I had a video conference scheduled with the mayor's team to "win" the contract that we'd paid for. The FBI wanted to participate. The only problem was, I could not call in sick due to being short on staff. So that meant the FBI agents had to come to my job for the call. Thankfully, the city we were having the meeting with was on the East Coast, and the meeting was scheduled for 9 a.m. their time, which meant it was 6 a.m. our time. I would not have too many customers at the office at that time. The FBI agents and I planned for an early morning briefing at 5:45 a.m. on September 24 at my Berkeley office before the video conference meeting with the City of New Haven. New Haven was three hours ahead of us. The agents needed to be there to witness this Zoom meeting.

We set up the video camera so it would only show me. On the other side of the table were FBI agents listening, recording, and taking notes. They wanted me to intentionally throw the meeting. For example, one of the requirements for the contract with New Haven was that Government App Solutions be headquartered in their city. So, my answer was, "No, but if it makes you guys happy we can just get a post office box there for a few days and then cancel it after you issue the contract." The reasoning behind this was to clearly show the company was not qualified, nor did not meet the requirements; however, I knew the city would still issue us the contract because of the bribe.

This was a common practice method we used to clearly capture elected officials directing contracts to us in quid pro quos. More importantly, it was helpful to be able to see who the mayors were directing to help them carry out their corruption. It would be these people, who directly reported to the mayor, that the FBI would reach out to and strike agreements with to help us catch the mayor and uncover other crimes.

After several months of working with WeWork and Mayor Johnson, he was confident I was solid and loyal to him. As the time progressed, I would voluntarily help him with challenges and tasks he needed to get done. However, his paranoia was still around. He would constantly change cell phones and numbers. Every time he did this, we would have to call him and have an FBI agent confirm a visual pickup from him.

FBI agents doing a visual phone pick up confirmation was a common practice in all the cases I worked. The reason was that a lot of politicians often escaped prosecution by stating that they were not the actual one sending and receiving messages from others on their cell phones; it was their aides. So, we would generally have to get an agent undercover next to the target, or across the street recording at the moment I would call, to show that it was the target picking up that specific phone at that specific number.

For Kevin, although he was trying to stay out of the spotlight, yet another scandal would soon appear. Through Kevin and Michelle's efforts trying to open a Lo-Lo's Chicken & Waffles soul food franchise restaurant in downtown Sacramento, they were both required to frequently travel to Las Vegas for training.

While at training, Kevin allegedly started having an affair with a much younger server. When another employee told the owner and showed him pictures that Kevin was sending her colleague, the owner flipped out and booted Kevin and his wife out of the program. The restaurant chain canceled Kevin's franchise. Instead of cutting his losses, he and Michelle decided to open their own soul food restaurant, Fixins Soul Kitchen, in the same location where the Lo-Lo's Chicken & Waffles location had been planned to go.

During the investigation into Kevin, a lot of things became apparent to me. The dots were starting to connect, and it became undeniable that Kevin was a criminal and had a major sex problem. He loved to take advantage of people. Having been a victim of this in my childhood years, I was determined to fight back and help take down this monster. I remember all those times as a child I felt helpless and defeated, not knowing how to fight and get away from my babysitter, who would molest me day after day, week after week.

CHAPTER TWELVE

AMERICORPS

During the course of this investigation, in late 2019, the FBI received direction from Washington to look into a few matters relating to Kevin, the AmeriCorps investigation, and NBA officials. The objective was to bring these matters up to see what we could get Kevin to disclose. The agents had intercepted some communications regarding yet another closed-door deal to keep the Sacramento Kings basketball team in Sacramento. In addition, they now had new information regarding Kevin and his high-level connections, who had gotten his previous AmeriCorps investigation closed. Now, people were requesting repayment of these favors.

In 2004, Kevin had illegally directed AmeriCorps funds to his personal nonprofit, St. HOPE Academy in Sacramento. After the scandal was uncovered, AmeriCorps decided not to pursue charges, fired the inspector general who had uncovered it, and then invited Kevin Johnson back as a speaker!

Kevin Johnson had arranged to be awarded a grant from AmeriCorps for a little less than $1 million. It was a three-year grant awarded to St. HOPE, Kevin's charter school he had established. St. HOPE claimed the money was going to be used for the community. It stated that the grant's purpose was to "revitalize inner-city communities through public education, civic leadership, economic development, and the arts."[1]

However, in 2008, the inspector general for AmeriCorps investigated the use of the funds and found that Kevin Johnson had spent almost half on his personal expenses. After federal prosecutors investigated this matter, they only ordered Kevin and St. HOPE to pay back about half of the grant it had received.

When Kevin was mayor of Sacramento and trying to direct a RAILS grant to one of my companies in a quid pro quo, I had asked him about this situation. I told him that it would seem to be rolling the dice due to the AmeriCorps allegations which had been made against him and his organization. And because he was in the middle of purchasing stock to become an owner in the company with me, I did not want to get caught up with negative publicity in the media or be the subject of a potential investigation.

One night at his house, I remember us specifically having a conversation about this.

"Hey, Derek, I got you," he would say.

"Yeah. But what if they see that you're an owner?"

"We'll just hold my stock until I leave office. Then after, you can give me the shares. We'll put something in writing with Kevin [Heistand—Kevin Johnson's longtime friend and attorney] and then figure it out later."

"Okay. You don't think it'll come up again, or that anyone who doesn't win will get suspicious and start looking into things?"

"Nah. We took care of all those guys. They are no longer there. They wanted to act up and not follow orders, so they got booted. Everyone else knows better, and they aren't going to challenge us."

"Okay. I'll get back to you shortly about it."

However, I knew better. I backed out of the grant deal. It was not a gamble I was willing to take. It was too early for me, and I just did not know a lot about it. Nonetheless, I did investigate the matter more. I found that officials at the Corporation for National and Community

Service (CNCS), which oversees AmeriCorps, had banned Kevin Johnson from receiving any more federal dollars. Then they had almost immediately removed the funding ban. It had been removed in 2009, when Sacramento officials expressed the fear that it might prevent the city from receiving millions of dollars in federal stimulus money.

Ironically enough, Kevin Johnson was then asked to speak at the National Conference on Volunteering and Service, which is the parent company of AmeriCorps! The news of Kevin's speaking position in an AmeriCorps/CNCS event struck Gerald Walpin, the inspector general who uncovered Johnson's wrongdoing and was then fired, as astonishing. Walpin was quoted as saying, "This is worse than finding a fox in the chicken coop. This is inviting the fox in and honoring him."[2] Again, shocking for most of us. However, it was nothing but another morning for Kevin Johnson.

But the former inspector general was not going to go down without a fight. In a public comment, he made the following statement.

CNCS itself made the finding less than two years ago that Kevin Johnson could not be trusted with AmeriCorps grants because of the undisputed facts that established his personal misuse of those funds. On that basis, CNCS suspended Johnson from access to any further federal funds. While political pressure caused CNCS to lift that suspension, the findings remain findings made by CNCS, and the suspension, never rescinded, remains a blot on Johnson's reputation. To now award Johnson with the honor of being a featured speaker at AmeriCorps' National Conference demonstrates CNCS's continued lack of comprehension of its responsibility to separate itself from those who have misused taxpayers' money. Moreover, it sends the wrong message to the AmeriCorps staff, members, and grantees in spotlighting Johnson as exemplifying how grantees should be run. You can be certain that if I had not unlawfully been removed from my IG position, the IG's Office would have made, loud and clear, its objection to this unacceptable invitation.[3]

Nonetheless, Walpin was fired from his job by President Barack Obama without giving the required 30-day notice to Congress and stating the reasons therein. Democratic leaders stated that they were concerned the law was not followed—a law was created in June 2009 to protect inspector generals from being fired without the appropriate notice, warning, or explanation. Some noted that there was a clear conflict of interest due to the face that Mayor Kevin Johnson and President Barack Obama were close friends. Senators from both parties (Democrat and Republican) came together to send a letter to Congress expressing concern regarding the response they had received from the administration regarding the lack of the required notice, and the short and vague answer provided for firing Inspector General Walpin. It was amazing power Kevin had from the bottom to the top politicians. He could always get someone to intervene on his behalf.

Unfortunately, the former Inspector General Walpin started to fight and tried to bring this matter to light on several occasions. One day, just as he was planning and preparing to file another lawsuit, he was struck by a passing car crossing the street and died.

CHAPTER THIRTEEN
DESTROYING THE UNITED BLACK MAYORS ORGANIZATION

The National Conference of Black Mayors (NCBM) is an excellent example of the totality of Kevin Johnson's reach. This national government sector lobbying association was founded in 1974 after the Civil Rights Act of 1964 and the Voting Rights Act of 1965 were enacted. At the association's height, the group represented about 650 African American mayors across the United States. According to the defunct website, the mission was focused on strengthening local leadership through redevelopment of the nation's most vulnerable communities.

Kevin Johnson was named president of the nonprofit in 2013, and immediately, issues arose. There were concerns regarding how he was elected, about his ownership in a charter school system, and that he was trying to remove the executive director. In a presentation to the group, created by Kevin's team within the city, the word "coup" was used, which caused some members to become leery of his real motives and intentions. A little more than a month after Kevin was elected NCBM president, the group's board ruled that his election was invalid because Kevin had not observed any of the election rules. He had been elected with a show of hands rather than with written ballots. There were other alleged violations, as well.

The NCBM was not a stranger to scandals, as previous conference president, George L. Grace Sr., former mayor of St. Gabriel, Louisiana, was sentenced to 22 years in federal prison for corruption, bribery, and other charges uncovered during an FBI sting operation called Operation Blighted Officials. However, in 2013, documents from the City of Sacramento, obtained through a public records request by a local reporter by the name of Cosmo Garvin under the California Public Records Act, showed things were looking up for the organization.

Kevin, along with the city, filed lawsuits preventing emails located on the city's servers (from Johnson's personal email account) from being released. Out of 113 emails withheld, in 2016, a Sacramento superior court judge ruled to allow the release of 75. The emails showed that NCBM Executive Director Vanessa R. Williams had finally secured a world summit of mayors and presidents of African descent in Bogota after years of courtship. The Colombian government even pledged $1.8 million for the event to take place; however, Kevin had other plans for the organization.

Emails would also showcase how involved he was in orchestrating the removal of Williams. Along with his staff, he intercepted and hijacked communication with the Colombian government to cancel the world summit, which immediately took the organization into financial distress. In another situation, he also sabotaged a 2014 conference in Bermuda, which would have brought at least $500,000 into the NCBM coffers. Claims of financial irregularities were tossed around. Kevin personally conducted at least one exit interview with Williams's staff to collect information.

The chaos that ensued pitted mayors against mayors, causing them to have to make quick decisions about whether to support the executive director. These were tough decisions, considering the clout Kevin Johnson had. Making the wrong choice could and most likely would end political careers. Still, 14 mayors decided to support Williams.

The NCBM opposed any legislation supporting charter school systems or the funding of charter schools through taxpayer monies. Kevin not only supported charter schools, he owned and managed one —a conflict of interest. The NCBM would eventually file a lawsuit claiming Johnson's only motivation in being president was to dismantle the organization for reasons that became clear as time went on. Unfortunately, the mayors who opposed him had few resources compared to what Kevin could bring to the table, in the sense of both money and allies. Little did they know that in just a few months, Kevin would become the President of the US Conference of Mayors.

Based on the claim of financial irregularities, the NCBM was eventually forced to file for bankruptcy, although the legitimacy of the bankruptcy filing was also challenged by members of the organization. Later, other mayors would allege that Kevin's ultimate goal was to dismantle the organization and start a new group, the African American Mayors Association (AAMA), a claim which had merit, considering Johnson had filed the incorporation paperwork one day after the bankruptcy paperwork for NCBM was filed.

The AAMA filing listed the headquarters as located on Pennsylvania Avenue in Washington, DC, just three blocks from the White House. According to documents obtained by journalists, the expensive office location was given to the new group by a former NCBM board member. Documents later released showed Kevin used Sacramento city employees to help him orchestrate the "coup."

Just like that, the NCBM ceased to exist, and the AAMA was born. Kevin brought along former NCBM sponsors and members of the NCBM to his new organization. He named himself president and placed Stephanie Mash Sykes, his director of governmental affairs, as the new executive director. He also attempted to personally resolve the matter with the former executive director, Vanessa R. Williams, outside of court.

The story illustrates the extent of Kevin's ruthlessness. Not only would he come in and stage a "coup" of a major political group, he would set out to completely destroy it and set up an entirely new organization. That was no easy feat, yet he pulled it off. He would go on to even bigger political achievements. Without any real detractors left to rein him in, he was able to use his new lobbying group, the AAMA, to push for charter school funding and set up the group to receive hundreds of thousands in grants from various companies. Many of those grants would also be given to his charter school.

Once he took the reins as the president of the US Conference of Mayors, he leveraged even more of his contacts to pull money into the AAMA. In 2014, Uber gave $50,000 to the organization. In turn, Kevin, as mayor of Sacramento, announced Uber was part of his city's new Cities 3.0 initiative and later had Uber's CEO speak at the US Conference of Mayors' annual event. Just prior to that announcement, Uber was named the official ride-sharing service of the Sacramento Kings.

Kevin touted his election as President of the US Conference of Mayors as a big boon for his hometown. The position made him a national figure and came with tremendous clout. "I have this platform and it can be an extension of what I'm doing in Sacramento,"[1] he said.

He met with then-President Barack Obama at the White House. In January 2015, he gave the State of the Cities address, broadcasted on C-SPAN, to more than 300 of the nation's mayors. He also gave a warm introduction to President Obama, who spoke at the conference. "He's a really cool dude . . . he's hip, he's a smooth president,"[2] Kevin said, as Obama took the podium and greeted Kevin with a warm embrace. Kevin was clearly at the top of his game. Unfortunately, this only broadcast and boosted Kevin's agenda (and pocketbook) for when he would leave office.

For Kevin, being president of the newly formed AAMA in conjunction with his presidency of the US Conference of Mayors provided him the national heft, the profile, and the connections he would later use for more sinister and corrupt purposes. The NCBM had tons of potential prior to Kevin's involvement. If both conferences, in Colombia and Bermuda, had taken place and brought in the revenue they were predicting, who knows what the organization could have accomplished? Instead, an organization with a longstanding history of over 40 years, rooted in helping impoverished communities, no longer existed. It was all because of one man's ability to see how the organization could help fulfill a much larger, self-serving plan that would personally sustain him for years to come.

CHAPTER FOURTEEN
A NATURAL

Throughout my time with the FBI, I was often called by other offices to join in some of their active political corruption investigations all over the nation. Word was getting out that I was doing a good job on all the cases I was working. Many FBI agents said that I was a real natural for this kind of work. In general, I quickly got the evidence needed under budget and within a fraction of the time allotted.

For example, there was one target I will call "Ted" (because this is an open investigation being prosecuted now, and this person is cooperating, so I cannot use the real name) who I had to partner with. He was involved in a mix of a quid pro quo and extortion deal with a mayor. The case file on this individual was so detailed that I not only knew what type of marijuana business he was involved in, but I knew his best product, favorite National Football League (NFL) team, and, more importantly, how much more money and partnerships he needed to make it big.

So, after studying the research, I was inserted into the investigation. I was given 30 days to try to create a bond with Ted, and, more importantly, engage myself in his business. It took me only one night at the bar. I walked in wearing an NFL jersey of not only his favorite team, but his favorite player on the team, and grabbed a seat close to him at the bar. I was using an alias name, saying I happened to be visiting in town wrapping up things for my brother, who had just passed away.

My story was I was going to be coming into some more money and figured it would be great to honor my brother by doing some business in the City of Fall River. However, I only knew about the cannabis business and was not so sure that was even allowed in Fall River.

"Go Chiefs!" I heard from the side of me.

I smiled. Line in the water, and the fish took the bite.

"All day, baby!" I said.

"How's it going?" Ted asked.

"Pretty good. Didn't think that I would see any Chiefs fans in this town," I said.

"Oh yeah. I'm a diehard fan. Grew up there and then moved out this way when my parents split."

"No kidding. Have you been keeping up with them?"

"Hell yeah. Patrick Mahomes totally deserved MVP. And how about that Super Bowl?" he said.

"Right," I said.

The funny thing was, I did not watch football. It was never my thing. I have probably only watched four or five games in my entire life. However, for this operation, I had to do a lot of research to prepare to meet this target and create a strong bond.

We would spend the rest of the night at the bar talking sports, and then I led the conversation into business. I told him I was in the cannabis industry and was thinking about expanding.

"No way. I'm in the middle of opening up shop here in Fall River," he said.

"Get the fuck out of here. Really?"

"We gotta talk. We might be able to do something," he said.

And just like that, I was in. I could study the targets' files, quickly assess what drove them and their passions, and then insert myself to fit into them, reaching their bigger life picture and goals. In the end, I figured all this could only help me with my own legal case.

All the investigations I assisted on were unique. They centered around politicians, who are generally hard people to get next to. However, I had several ways to get close to them. I could use one of my own political connections, which meant I would be going under my real name. I could use one of the FBI's connections, who was either an already elected politician or another confidential human source working the politician. Getting introduced to the politician who was under investigation was always easy and would lead to me being welcomed with open arms when successfully done. Then, it was on to business, the normal play.

However, as I spent more and more time on this case, it really made me scratch my head. It involved a mayor not too much younger than me—Jasiel Correia II. He was the mayor of Fall River, Massachusetts. He was a mayor who was indicted in October 2018 on one federal case, and then found himself in the middle of another federal investigation on a completely different matter, leading to another separate indictment. It was a head scratcher. Did he think he was invisible? Well, I could not blame him after hearing his rebound story.

After he was indicted the first time, the city held a special election to have him removed and elect a new mayor for Fall River. Yet, even though he was under indictment and facing other legal troubles, the great people of Fall River reelected him. Only in America.

The back story on Mayor Correia II was that he was previously a tech entrepreneur and had allegedly made some poor choices by taking money from his startup investors and using it to fund his lavish lifestyle. The US Attorney's Office and the FBI had proof that Correia had spent over $200,000 of the money his company, SnoOwl, had received from investors on himself. He could have possibly wiggled out of this one had it not been for him telling the investors he would forgo paying himself a salary, and not reporting the money he took on his taxes. So, the government indicted him.[1]

Shockingly, after bailing out of custody, and knowing that the federal government (including the FBI and the IRS) had been investigating him, the FBI (while still monitoring him and his close circle) intercepted a text message from one of the mayor's aides. It was a text to a marijuana company that had promised money in exchange for the mayor to issue non-opposition letters to do business and legally operate in Fall River—allegedly. The aide was texting the company to see why it was taking so long to pay $150,000.

Now, this was an opportunity for the FBI. When people are short on money, they often start to shortcut due diligence and other processes. They just tend to focus on the endgame, which is getting money. Insert a confidential human source, who happens to be an entrepreneur and investor on the side, and I could walk right in. The objective was to become a major stakeholder in the company, get close with the founders, and get in on the communication between them, the mayor, and his team.

Out of the several companies the mayor was allegedly extorting money from, I was only involved with two of them. Once the mayor found out the company I was working with now had more money, due to my investment and partnership, it was, like they say, as easy as stealing candy from a baby.

The US Attorney's Office had little patience for this guy. Once the attorneys reviewed all the evidence that had been collected, they decided to go ahead and instruct the agents to take down the case. Because Mayor Correia II was not a violent person and did not fight or resist arrest in his first federal indictment, there was not a big takedown planned. Plus, there were a few other individuals who needed to get picked up.

The team had a quick briefing and then headed out to go arrest Mayor Correia II. No tactical gear or anything, just plain clothes. The government had noticed that over the past few years, because Mayor Correia II allegedly stole hundreds of thousands of dollars from investors, he had started living a lavish lifestyle—buying a Mercedes-Benz, fancy designer clothes, and expensive jewelry.

After being arrested, the court released Correia on a $25,000 bond. Now with both cases over his head, Correia II is facing stiff jail time. After the second indictment, the people of Fall River decided, "Fool me once, shame on you. Fool me twice, shame on me."

The charge of wire fraud provides for a sentence up to 20 years in prison. Filing false tax returns provides for a sentence up to three years in prison. Extortion conspiracy provides for a sentence up to 20 years. Extortion, aiding, and abetting provides for a sentence up to 20 years. Bribery charges provide for a sentence up to ten years.[2]

Hopefully Jasiel Correia II will be honest, stop costing taxpayers more money by having the government prosecute this case, and confess, take a plea and finally start putting this matter behind him.

CHAPTER FIFTEEN
THE LIFE OF AN FBI SOURCE

During the investigations I participated in for over two years, I began to get burned out. The WeWork job really took a lot out of me, and I wanted to return to my own case and get it resolved. Furthermore, I felt a growing concern that the FBI was specifically targeting the Democratic party. During the course of all the investigations I was working, both Republicans and Democrats were being implicated. However, the Bureau was only truly interested in pursuing the Democrats. More importantly, I was being directed to issue campaign donations via gift cards to Republican candidates, who were "allegedly" under investigation, and then after all the donations were made, the "investigation" was dropped. Then I came to find that these were not even on the books. It was too much for me. I had already fulfilled my obligation and was now just in overtime.

One of my biggest concerns when debating whether I should help the FBI in its efforts to take down political corruption was the various stories I had previously heard. In 2018, I did not have a clue as to whether these stories were true. However, I had seen a famous case regarding a confidential human source the FBI used and then threw under the bus. It was the story of Richard Wershe Jr., depicted in the 2018 movie, *White Boy Rick.*

Rick Wershe was an independent contractor for the FBI at the age of 14, and worked for the FBI for several years. After the relationship with the FBI and Rick started to sour, the FBI agents backdated some paperwork and changed things around to throw Rick under the bus and save their own careers. However, this was later exposed, and Rick's charges and sentence were changed. Initially, he was sentenced to life in prison. This was something I had to pay attention to and balance in my consideration of whether to work with the FBI. At the same time, I had to remember that it was just a movie based on true events.

On the other hand, there was another famous case, one with a much better ending. It was the case of Frank Abagnale Jr., a career criminal who started committing crimes at the age of 15. In 2020, he is working as an independent contractor for the FBI. In his early life, he impersonated an attorney, a pilot, and a law enforcement officer. When the FBI finally caught up with him, it realized he had a true talent.

Frank was arrested and sentenced; however, he was asked to work for the FBI for the remainder of his prison sentence. Frank still works for the FBI, but now as a partner. He owns his own fraud protection and cybersecurity company and provides services to the FBI while also teaching new recruits at the FBI's training camp (best known as Quantico). Frank's case was so unique, like the movie *White Boy Rick,* that *Catch Me If You Can* also became a hit movie.

I figured I had a 50-50 chance of this going well. Nonetheless, I would be sure to build a few back doors, and make sure to take my normal precautions, just in case it came down to "he said, she said." As things progressed with the cases we were investigating, we had our ups and downs. Sometimes, we did not know what was going on and why things would stall. I would be lying if I did not say that during one or two of those times, I believed I could have been in danger.

One day, the agents and I were discussing our next steps. My motivation was low as I was genuinely concerned about my safety. Then, our conversation changed, and it caught my attention and made me become instantly more motivated.

This occurred one day when Special Agent Bills said, "I'm working on getting your charges dropped."

Life stood still at that point.

"Really?" I asked.

"Yeah. I still must have a conversation with the US attorney to get him onboard, but when I mentioned it briefly to him, he was not opposed. But you need to continue to perform. And you will have to agree to work with us for at least five years," she said.

"Absolutely," I said. I was even more determined.

This was a true game-changer. Having my entire case dropped would be huge. I could finally put this chapter behind me and move on with my life. However, on the other hand, I knew there would be more the FBI would want from me.

Over the course of the following weeks, I would occasionally ask Special Agent Bills if there were any updates or progress on getting my charges dropped. She would say no, and that the timing just was not right. After almost a month of this, I decided to go a different route and tell my attorney about it to see if he could reach out to the US Attorney's Office and get some direction.

When I initially reached out to my attorney and told him what the agent had told me, he laughed. He tried to assure me that the agent was only pulling a quick one on me and had no intention to try to get my case dropped.

This infuriated me at first. Then it made me think. Was Special Agent Rebekah Bills just using this as an opportunity to work me further? How would this play out? Again, thankfully, I had taken measures to prove that I had been told this, should it ever be disputed.

My attorney agreed to reach out to the US attorney in charge and schedule a meeting. He would also try to see if I could get a read from the US attorney in the morning, as he was scheduled to see him at court regarding another client who had a hearing scheduled. He said that he would call me after talking to him.

The next morning, I received a call from my attorney shortly after 11 o'clock. He had just spoken with the US attorney and said they agreed to have a meeting the next day at the US Attorney's Office. He also said that when the US attorney asked him what the meeting would be regarding, he replied it was following up about the FBI's request to have my case dropped. The US attorney looked shocked and said that he did not believe that was the direction they were going to be heading. However, we should all get together and discuss it.

Again, I was infuriated. Was Special Agent Bills lying to me? Should I bring proof to the meeting, showing she was the one who had proposed this? I calmed myself and decided to wait until the meeting to see exactly what would happen and how things would play out.

Later that night, as I was winding down, my phone rang. I could see from the caller identification that it was Special Agent Bills. I decided to let it roll over to voicemail. I was in no mood to talk right then, and I feared it was going to be a pep talk to say, "Hey, I need more time," or some excuse.

The next morning as I was heading to meet with my attorney to go to the US Attorney's Office, my phone went off again. It was Special Agent Bills. This time I knew she was calling to talk to me about the meeting that was about to take place. I started to get butterflies.

My attorney and I headed to the US Attorney's Office. After we exchanged pleasantries and greetings, we got straight to business. My attorney said, "As you know, Mr. Bluford initially came on board to help the government capture evidence against Kevin Johnson. Within a few weeks, the FBI valued Mr. Bluford and his unique set of skills and access and asked him if he would consider coming on board for other investigations, cases, and operations. He agreed. Since then, he has been doing a great job. I have heard this consistently from the FBI agents, the US Department of Justice, and your offices. It appears that the FBI has now informed my client that it is going to try to get his case dropped. In return, Mr. Bluford would commit himself to work for the FBI for five years. So, here we are."

The room was silent. It just so happened that conveniently, Special Agent Bills was unable to make it to the meeting. They said she had to leave town at the last minute, as something had come up. The US attorney in charge looked at the AUSA who oversaw my case and then looked at me.

"Mr. Bluford, you have been doing an amazing job. We are all beyond amazed at the work that you have been doing. A few things, though. What has been communicated to you has not been communicated to us. Furthermore, the FBI has no right to make those kinds of promises or imply such things. It has no legal right or control over the outcome of your case. Only we do. Unfortunately, we do have a case, and we will all work together to resolve yours. Everything that you are doing only helps you."

Well, that surely was not the answer I was looking for. But, before deciding to take this case in a whole new direction and completely pull out, I had to ask a question to make sure I was not being intentionally screwed over.

"Mr. Anderson, did Special Agent Bills ever even ask you to have my case dropped?" I asked.

"No. She did not," he said.

And there it was. I was being used. Oh, this would not turn out how anyone expected.

"I find it interesting that Special Agent Bills is not available for this meeting," said my attorney.

"Well, we actually have her on the line. Hold on," said US Attorney Michael Anderson.

He then pressed a few buttons on the conference phone in the room.

"Agent Bills, are you there?" he said.

"Yes," said Agent Bills.

"We have Derek and his attorneys here, Amy, and me. How are you doing?"

"Good. Thanks. Hi, everyone. Sorry I couldn't be there. Something came up at the office," she said.

I smiled. They did not even have their stories straight. She said something came up at the office, however, the US attorney had said she had to go out of town. *Here it comes.*

"Agent Bills, we know you are busy, so we won't take up a lot of your time. Mr. Bluford is under the impression that you are pushing for his charges to be dropped. Can you provide some more information?"

"Yeah. Derek, you have been doing a great job. But when you asked me to do this, the reason I kept putting it off was because I can't. I have no control over these things," she said.

My heart dropped. What? Did she just say, "When I asked her to do this"? When did I ever ask her? My blood began to boil. Okay. *This is the way you are going to do me,* I thought. *Big mistake.* Now, everything was off. I would surely stand my ground, and everyone would remember this. I had to slow my thinking. I had to calm down. I had to think.

I knew that at this point, I could simply walk away from helping. I had legally fulfilled my obligation and the court would grant the 5K1 motion to reduce my sentence significantly. However, my anger got the best of me. I had reverted from everything I had been learning over the past year in my MRT program.

My problem was, I always tried to teach people lessons. If they tried to take advantage of me or someone I cared about, I would always go to extreme efforts to prove a point or teach them a lesson. However, through MRT, I learned that I had to let this go. I had to make peace with it, and, more importantly, I had to accept that it was not my right or job to do. However, the ironic thing was that everything I was learning not to do through MRT, I was being forced to do through my legal agreement with the government. I was legally obligated to lie, mislead, manipulate, and break the law at the direction of the FBI.

So, I said, "Fuck it." She had put my life in danger so many times and caused me to jump through all these hoops. To now not come through and help me was wrong. I would surely have to take steps to make sure that Special Agent Bills could never do this to anybody again. She did not deserve to be an FBI agent.

About the time I came back around, everyone was looking at me, waiting for an answer. The US Attorney's Office knew I was an important witness and asset for its cases. Special Agent Bills knew the same thing. She had taken a big gamble overseeing all the cases against leading politicians. One mistake and she would be out of a job. Yet, she'd rolled the dice.

"Okay. Thanks. It must have been my misunderstanding," I said.

I do not think anyone was buying into that answer.

"Okay. Well, thanks for your time, Agent Bills. We are going to wrap up with Derek," AUSA Michael Anderson said.

As a side note, to make things even more interesting, from time to time, Special Agent Bills would get suspicious of me due to the way I was saying things and prompting confirmation. She would occasionally stop and ask me, throughout my time working with the FBI, "Bluford, are you recording us?"

"No," I would say. "That is illegal."

The fact of the matter was, yes, it is generally illegal to record people in California without their consent. However, if someone were to hire counsel in New York, which is a one-party consent state, and then call the counsel every time they would meet up with people, then it would be okay for that counsel to record the conversation. Additionally, in California, you are allowed to record authorities, police and people acting in public office. This is all just hypothetical, of course, though.

Back at the meeting, AUSA Anderson said, "Derek, is there anything you want to talk about? We are all here and can figure something out."

What do I do? Should I tell him the truth? No, he must already know the truth. Agent Bills had promised something she either had no intention of ever delivering, or she had been shut down by the AUSA when she mentioned it. Nonetheless, I came to the conclusion that they were not on my side.

"No. I'm fine. You have a good day," I said.

Then I looked at my attorney and shook my head to motion I was ready to leave. As I was leaving, I could tell everyone had "oh, shit" looks on their faces.

We then all shook hands and walked out.

As we got into the elevator, my attorney said, "Derek, just breathe. Don't do anything rash."

As I had feared, my case was not being dropped. That day, it had merely been used to motivate me and to get me back on point. I was infuriated. I kept thinking, *What should I do?* It was portrayed as if I had asked for this favor, and that was not the way it had happened at all. Having a degree in law, I knew that an agent could not dismiss my case and that it could only happen through the US Attorney's Office. Therefore, I would have never asked someone I knew did not have authority to do what I knew they could not do. It would have been like asking a cat to recite a poem . . . it was not going to happen. However, given all the time we had been working together and building a relationship, I wanted to trust her. I wanted to believe her. Why would she risk throwing it all away?

By the time I got outside of the US Attorney's Office, I was in a destructive mood. If I was going to be screwed over and made a fool of, then so would everyone else. Building back doors had always been my specialty. Did they think I had not prepared for such an occasion? They knew I always recorded everything. They had been downloading my phone frequently and knew I had a video on it of one of our meetings, which I'd intentionally left on there. I had caught everything. The mistakes, the direction to handicap a certain political party, and, more importantly, the personal vendettas of those involved in the investigation. One call to my attorney in New York—I was certain that would fix it all.

However, I knew it would be best to wait until the indictments came. Then there would be no reverse. Always wait and let them step into it first.

I would need to appear to be angry and not respond to Special Agent Bills, Agent La'Chappelle, or the US Attorney's Office for a few days. Have them continue to try to reach out to me and "convince" me to continue. Then, I would. And I would be sure to start building back doors for all the cases. If she did not come clean at the end, then all the cases would be destroyed.

CHAPTER SIXTEEN
NEW HAVEN

fter two weeks of dodging calls and text messages from Special Agent Rebekah Bills, I finally responded and agreed to meet up with her one night at Starbucks.

"Hey, are you okay?" she asked.

"No. Not really," I said.

"Derek, I think you have had so much going on, and you've been being pulled in so many different ways that you really misheard what I had said."

Motherfucker, I was thinking. *You think you are that good that you are going to seriously try to get me to doubt myself. Okay. I will play along.*

"I don't know," I said.

"Derek, remember, there have been some times where you thought you caught something on one of our recordings, and it wasn't there. I think you have just had so much on your plate, and that is my fault. So, I apologize. Now, are you going to leave me hanging, or are you going to help me wrap up these cases?" she asked.

Oh, don't you worry. I'm going to help you wrap up these cases all right, I thought.

"All right, Rebekah. But let's hurry up and get this over with," I told her.

Special Agent Bills then began to converse with me regarding some personal things we both had shared with each other while working together. She gave me some updates about her son, and I told her about my life. She even told me that the special agent in charge had given her permission to just come kidnap my ass if I had not responded to her tonight. This was not uncommon. Indirect and direct threats had become a norm.

During the two weeks I had been dodging her, Kevin had finally heard from one of mayors to get things back on track for the contract in exchange for campaign contributions. This was good news. The FBI and I turned our attention to New Haven, Connecticut, where Toni Harp was the mayor. She had previously tried to give our company a contract with the city in return for cash and a promise to contribute to her next mayoral campaign.

However, one thing Kevin did not know was we already had his phones tapped. When Mayor Harp called Kevin, I just happened to be with him, and I knew the FBI was listening.

"Kevin, how are things going?" she asked.

"Good, Mayor. Thanks for putting things together for me. It appears that things are getting back on track," Kevin said.

"Yes. You said you were going to get me campaign funds as long as I get you this contract," Harp said.

"Yes, Mayor."

"I need at least $25,000, minimum. When can you get out here?"

Kevin looked at me and covered the phone while asking, "Can you do next week?"

I said, "Yes."

"I'm sending him [meaning me] next week," Kevin told Mayor Harp.

This was good. This was more progress.

I then went to the FBI office and we arranged my travel to New

Haven to meet with the mayor, and, of course, the FBI joined me. However, we weren't only flying out for the Mayor Harp investigation. There would be another politician who I would be visiting, one who was holding a campaign event about two hours away. Over the next several days, we ironed out the meeting details for both operations.

Previously, the same situation had happened in New Haven as in Los Angeles. The mayor had promised us a contract, but then the parking director pushed back and caused us all to put things on hold. Doug Hausladen, who served as the parking director, believed there was something fishy about us and the city. I remember Doug saying, "Something is not right here. The mayor shouldn't be directing me to do something that is my decision."

"You need to check with the mayor," I replied. "This is happening. We have already started planning for this."

Then Doug sent an email to the city attorney, copying me, asking him to investigate. The city attorney agreed with the parking director that we were not following the proper legal bidding process. As a result, things were put off for some time. That would be until the mayor's campaign for reelection came up.

We set up shop at a local hotel and came up with a plan. Special Agent Bills identified what we needed to confirm and hear from my meeting with Mayor Harp. We needed a clear quid pro quo, meaning she would give us the city contract if we gave her money. Again, this was clearly illegal, and would result in an easy prison sentence of several years.

I arrived at Mayor Harp's campaign headquarters right on time. I walked in and introduced myself to her staff. Everyone was nice. After all, I was a donor. It was only seconds until Mayor Harp appeared and summoned me to the back office.

"How are you doing, Rick?" Mayor Harp asked. I was then going by Rick Bluford. It was best, because if someone were to look for Derek Bluford online, they would see that I was currently indicted. If they searched for Rick or Richard, nothing would come up relating to me.

"I am doing well, Mayor. How are you doing?" I asked her.

"Stressed. This campaign is driving me crazy," she said.

"I am sorry to hear this."

"Look, I am in a bit of a rush, so forgive me for being direct. We need to raise money fast. I know you need a contract with the city, and it just makes sense for us to work together on this. I know last time we had a little problem with Doug, but trust me, that will not happen this time. You'll get the contract if you can help my campaign," she said.

"How much do you need?" I asked her.

"I'm short $70-80,000," she replied.

"We can definitely contribute to that, but you need to assure me about the contract," I said.

"Yes. I'll get Doug and Daryl to move this through fast. Let's get together for dinner tonight or tomorrow," she said.

"Okay."

The meeting was fast and successful. However, we needed to slow things down just a bit. I reached out to Mayor Harp and asked her for another meeting with the parking department with her there. She agreed and set the meeting for the next day.

At the meeting, Mayor Harp introduced me to her team and told them they would be working with my company for parking enforcement. She then told Doug, the parking director, who had thrown everything off last time, to get it done. Doug immediately asked for references. However, we were not sure which ones to give.

The FBI wanted me to reach out to Kevin and see what he suggested. So, once we got back to the hotel, I called him.

"Hey, Kevin, how's it going?"

"Good, D. Harp texted me and said she's on top of things. How was the meeting?"

"It went pretty good. Just ran into a minor problem with fuckin' Doug, of course."

"Need me to hit the mayor? What happened?"

"He said he needed to talk to some references about this specific program."

"Oh. That is no problem. I'll have a few city mayors call him and say we are providing their cities with this same program and that it's a great service, and that they've seen an increase in revenue, efficiency, and a decrease in cost. I'll have Stockton, Phoenix, and a few others from our list hit them. Will that work?"

"Yeah."

At first, I was doubtful this would happen. How and why would city mayors, or any city staff for that matter, take a chance sending emails and making calls to another city and lie about another company? Especially because if someone wanted to investigate the matter to verify it, they could. But, as always, Kevin made it happen. He even had me send an introduction email to Stockton representatives and to Doug.

In the end, cities we had not even met with called Doug, emailed him, and gave letters of recommendation for our company. Doug was defeated at this point and had to move things along.

Now, because Mayor Harp was showing commitment and signs of coming through, it was time to pay the piper. Mayor Harp once again requested we have dinner later that night. I agreed.

We went to a nice steakhouse in downtown New Haven. The FBI was on all three corners, listening. The mayor showed up with her two right-hand people: Andrea Scott and Daryl Jones, the city controller. We had dinner and enjoyed some conversation relating to Kevin, the way he worked, her past, the US Conference of Mayors, and her wins as mayor of New Haven. Then it came down to business.

"Kevin said that you guys could do $25,000 ASAP," Mayor Harp said.

"Yes. I have already contributed a couple thousand dollars online, and I have another couple thousand cash on me. Can you produce some names and contribute it?" I asked.

The FBI agents had decided we should show some good faith early on and make some online donations to Harp's campaign as part of the bribe. However, they did not want to use any of the agents' names in case Kevin asked me. So, the FBI directed me to use some of my family and friends' names. The FBI would buy all the gift cards and use those card numbers to make the online donations. For others, we would send them money directly so they could make the contributions online.

"Yeah," Mayor Harp replied.

She then took the envelope of cash I had. Little did she know that the FBI was watching, and that it was filled with FBI dollars in marked bills. However, our meeting had gone on so long that the live feed battery had died out. So, the FBI was no longer able to hear and see what was going on in real time. The agents would have to wait until I finished the meeting to collect the other video recording devices from me and download them.

"Mayor Harp, I am trusting that Doug will not be a problem for us again?"

"He's not going to be a problem this time, I assure you," the mayor said. We captured all of this on audio and video.

When I drove back to the meeting spot with the FBI agents, everyone was tired and ready for bed. However, they all wanted to debrief me right then and listen to the devices in the morning. As soon as I got in the car, we jumped into it.

"How did it go?" Special Agent Bills asked.

"It went all right," I said.

"How was dinner?"

"It was great. How was yours?"

"You mean the fast food and snacks we all ate while scrunched in a car recording you from across the street, watching you eat a nice steak?" she asked.

We all laughed.

"Well, I do have some good news," I said.

"What?" asked Special Agent Bills.

"She took the cash," I told them.

"What?!" both special agents said in unison.

At this point, they had not been not sure the mayor of New Haven would be so brave (or foolish) as to accept a cash contribution in public, from a known government services guy and with the people who she had with her.

"Get the fuck out of here!" said the other special agent.

We all had a moment . . . mouths were open.

"I told you. These people are brave. They think they are gods. They think that they can't be caught," I said.

"Okay. Let's get the recording devices off you. We are going to run to the local FBI office to watch the videos and then we'll come back," said Special Agent Bills.

Everyone was now wide awake and full of energy. As they were taking the audio and video recording devices off me, Special Agent Bills asked, "Who took the money from you?"

"Mayor Harp," I replied.

More shocked faces and smiles.

They soon took off to the local FBI office in downtown New Haven and returned almost an hour later. Everyone was happy. This operation was over. Now to head back to the West Coast and start getting the remaining payments made.

Early the following week, we ran into another problem. Although the politicians we were investigating often wanted us to funnel the money to them by contributing to their campaigns, the US Department of Justice raised red flags because the FBI and other government entities are not allowed to actually influence the outcomes of races. We were pumping so much money through that it was affecting campaigns. We were helping corrupt individuals get elected. And now, we too were getting limits set by the Department of Justice for these investigations.

On top of that, Mayor Harp reached out and asked if we could use some of the cash we gave her and redirect it to the Working Families Party Political Action Committee (PAC). She was only able to find a few names she could deposit the funds under. She would send $7,000 back if we could direct it to the Working Families PAC for her.

Meanwhile, Washington was telling us we needed to slow down. The FBI had to delay some of the money it was giving me to be used as bribes to avoid flooding too much cash into Harp's campaign and other campaigns. I can remember Mayor Harp and others calling Kevin to complain about the delays in the campaign contributions I was supposed to be making.

We were all stressed. The FBI, the mayors, the campaign director, Kevin, and me. The FBI and I knew we had to come through on all of the commitments, and, at the same time not anger Kevin, because then he would not do any more favors for mayors, members of Congress, or other politicians. On the other hand, we had to try our best not to swing elections by giving candidates too much cash.

For reasons that might not be obvious, I cannot identify all the campaigns to which we contributed because some went on to win their elections, even though it bothers me knowing how close these races were. Also, these are still pending investigations.

It got tough at times. I would sometimes dread the calls from Kevin. It would be brief, stern, quick calls like, "The mayor wants you to honor your commitment. Honor your commitment." Meaning, I had committed to fund the mayor, and I needed to finish doing that now.

In the end, Mayor Harp came through on her promise and our deal. She awarded our company the contract with the city, and we were in business with the City of New Haven. The contract was a $14.8 million contract with New Haven for five years. To avoid questions from the New Haven city council, Mayor Harp and Daryl Jones elected to issue the company a five/six-month initial contract with the option to extend for five years.

We would receive about 18 percent of the $14.8 million and receive millions on top of that for services. Kevin, who made the introductions and orchestrated the deal, was scheduled to get 10 percent of the profits. Harp, though, was defeated for reelection.

Overall, Kevin made $1.5 million, and he did not even have to jump on a flight. He just made a few calls, sent some text messages, and just like that . . . he was a little better off. And he would only have to give Mayor Harp 5 percent of his earnings.

And it is often said that crime doesn't pay.

CHAPTER SEVENTEEN
CORRUPT PACS

Another part of the Mayor Harp and New Haven investigation came down to a few political action committees (PACs). Specifically, the Working Families Party PAC and the Urban Leadership Committee. The Working Families Party is a minor political party in the United States, founded in New York in 1998. There are active chapters in New York; Connecticut; Oregon; New Jersey; Maryland; Washington, DC; Pennsylvania; Wisconsin; Rhode Island; Nevada; West Virginia; New Mexico; Ohio; Texas; and Illinois.

This organization took the hard-earned money of people and was supposed to be distributing it to the best candidate fit for the job. However, during my interactions with the leaders, I saw it was quite the opposite. The FBI and I were working with a woman by the name of Lindsay Farrell, who served as the executive director of the Connecticut Working Families Party. Mayor Toni Harp agreed to pay the Working Families Party in exchange for getting its endorsement and using the organization to funnel money from me to them into her campaign in exchange for a contract with the city.

In September 2019, Lindsay Farrell and Andrea Scott (from Mayor

Harp's team) were reaching out to me via text inquiring about an update for sending money to Mayor Harp. The FBI wanted me to make sure I came off as skeptical and untrusting about the arrangement to pay off Mayor Harp through the Working Families Party, so I could get their confirmations on audio and video. We arranged to have back-to-back calls with Andrea and then Lindsay.

"Hi, Andrea. How's it going?" I asked.

"Good. How are you doing?" she replied.

"I'm good. Listen, I'm running short on time, but I wanted to get some clarification from you before I send this money. Are you sure that they are going to send this to Mayor Harp? I'm not trying to give my money to them, and then they go and give it to another candidate. I need Harp to win, so we can get this contract with the city" I said.

"I assure you it's all been worked out and Harp will get the money," Andrea confirmed.

"This is a lot of money. I'm going to need to talk to Harp to confirm, to make sure we get the contract, regardless of whether Working Families comes through or not," I said.

"That's perfectly fine," Andrea said.

I then spoke with Mayor Harp, and she confirmed she had worked out the deal with the Working Families Party, and assured me it would come through and not pull a quick one over on her. She then told me to contact one of the people who had been referenced at Working Families. I spoke with two or three representatives from this organization, which just goes to show how normal this payoff thing was—so many people were aware of it.

The FBI wanted to capture as many calls and videos as we could with this sting. The reasoning behind collecting so many pieces of the same or similar evidence that confirmed other evidence was so the US Attorney's Office could prosecute the case easily. If an attorney was able to get one piece of evidence thrown out, the US Attorney's Office had plenty more supporting evidence to use. After all, these were wealthy politicians, who would spare no cost to save their own.

I then called Lindsay.

"Hi, Lindsay. This is Rick Bluford. Mayor Harp told me to give you a call. How are you doing?"

"Hi, Mr. Bluford. I'm glad to finally connect with you. Thanks for the call. Yes. We are waiting for your payment," Lindsay said.

"Yes. I was just a little nervous and skeptical. I am not trying to give $10,000 to you, and then you turn around and give it to someone else. I see that you haven't endorsed anyone and that you are still active with other candidates," I told her.

"Nope. I can assure you she's getting the money. It's already been arranged. Harp told us about the contract you need, and the support you are willing to give. We can't say that publicly, but the deal is done," she said.

"Okayyyyy," I said hesitantly.

"Harp will get the money. She's already taken care of us, and we've arranged it so the funds will immediately go to her. It's going to happen. We do this all the time," she assured.

I smiled and said, "Okay." I knew this was enough for the FBI.

However, Lindsay continued. "Tell me more about your company."

"Well, it's a government support services technology company. We can provide most any type of technology solution that a government would need. From enforcement and management technology to billing and analytics, we can do it all."

"Okay. I would love to introduce you to some of our other mayors and candidates. I am sure they would be willing to work with you if you can support them also," Lindsay said.

"That sounds interesting. Yes. I'll follow up with you next time I'm in town," I said.

"Great. In the meantime, how do you plan to send the money? I believe there is going to be a $10,000 transaction and then a $7,000 one?" Lindsay asked.

"I'll mail the checks today."

This was great news for us and a true win. We were able to capture another important part of this investigation that would not only help prove our case but also hopefully lead to more investigations, arrests, and convictions. Once we arrested the individuals in Working Families, they would only benefit by helping us by testifying regarding our case and telling us who else they had been doing this for.

However, as I mentioned before, we could not send the $10,000 right away, due to the new direction of the Department of Justice (DOJ). For this specific case, the DOJ had directed us to wait until the primaries had been held before sending any more money.

So, as we were all scratching our heads at the FBI office trying to figure out a plan, something came to me. I came up with the idea to mail a business check from one of my companies. The reason I proposed this was because I knew the Working Families Party could not accept business checks for donations in that amount. Connecticut had special campaign rules, which did not allow some donations to come from businesses, but only from individuals. So, if I sent a business check, Working Families would have to return it to me and request I send a personal check. Nonetheless, it would buy a week, and the primaries were just a day or two away, so we could then turn over the funds.

When the Working Families Party received the business check, people were frustrated. I received calls from Mayor Harp, Andrea Scott, Lindsay, and even Kevin Johnson. Everyone erupted: "Why did you send a business check?!" I apologized and said, "Just send it back to me and I'll resend a personal check."

At this same time, Mayor Harp and Andrea Scott had mailed me a check for $7,000. This was because they could not find fake contributors and I had agreed to send that money to the Working Families Party. However, it was, of course, made out to my undercover name. I decided to deposit the check into my regular account, believing the bank would reject it due to the name mismatch.

Bingo! The bank rejected the check overnight and sent me an email about it. I was then able to play this off to Mayor Harp's team like they had written me a bad check. I sent them a copy of the email I had received from my bank and then asked, "What is going on?" They apologized and tried assuring me they had the funds in the account, and they were not sure why the check had been rejected. I did my best to come off as frustrated. We then came up with another solution for them to get me my money . . . well, the FBI's money. They said they would send it online to one of my merchant accounts. Once that was done, it had bought us enough time to make it to the primaries and send the additional money to Mayor Harp, laundered through the Working Families Party.

What are these PACs, such as Working Families, actually doing? Do the honest and hardworking people of America know how their donation money is being spent? What about the families and individuals who are donating to these organizations, hoping the money is going to go to their candidate if they "win" the endorsement? They have no clue their candidate never even had a chance for the endorsement because some backdoor deal had already been reached—that another candidate had actually bought the endorsement under the table. If the donors knew all this, would they still donate and support the PAC? How high does this go? Working Families Party has endorsed various mayors and even a former 2020 presidential candidate— who was wrongfully being pursued by the Bureau for political reasons.

As for the FBI, they said they just wanted to follow the money, which would lead them to corrupt organizations and politicians, leading to indict and arrest the guilty parties, and then give proffers to those who could lead us up the food chain—hopefully all the way to the top, to where the big fish swim.

CHAPTER EIGHTEEN
TENSION ESCALATES

In late January 2020, the main investigation was starting to end, at least for me. The FBI had me traveling the country for the past two years using many different aliases, titles, and companies, and they were starting to collide. Politicians and candidates were smart and often had the resources to run background checks, hire investigators, and track people. I had reached that point. Attorneys were starting to pull my case file, people were following me back to my hotels, my cars, and sending people to "bump into me" to meet me and hang out.

This was uncomfortable for me. I remember the first time the FBI alerted me that I was being followed. I had just left a meeting with a member of Congress and was heading back to the rendezvous location when I received a call.

"Derek, keep driving normally and don't look back. About three cars behind you, there is someone following you. We are right behind them," said the agent.

"Shit. What do I do?"

"Just keep driving and don't exit. We are going to have you drive to a shopping mall. Stand by. I will call you back."

"Fuckkkkk."

I had a million thoughts running through my head. *Are they armed? Do they know who I really am?* This was an investigation I had been working due to the FBI getting a tip. So, I was working it under an alias name. *What do they want? Are they going to try to grab me?* I had butterflies in my stomach and became nauseated. Thankfully, the agent called me back.

"Derek, put this address into your navigation," said the agent. She then gave me the information. "I want you to park and go into the mall to do some shopping. Under no circumstances do you look back or try to make out the driver or passengers of the car. We have other agents en route to the same location. You know I won't let anything happen to you."

"What? What's going on? I am really not liking this. Are you sure they are following me?" I asked.

"Yes. But I need you to focus. You can't let them know you are aware of their presence. After you park, leave the keys in the car cup holder."

Earlier, we had been working another congressperson who was demanding money in exchange for services—the exact quid pro quo we were going after. However, he was skeptical and was always questioning me and trying to find something inconsistent.

The FBI was made aware of him by someone who was dating a staffer of the congressman, not by the list Kevin had provided. The congressperson needed some funds due to a personal issue and had started meeting heavily with businesses to collect money in exchange for services. The staffer was upset about this and had voiced his concerns to his girlfriend, who in turn reported it to the FBI.

At the meeting I had just left, I was going to be handing over money to the congressperson. However, after taking it, he took a call and asked me for a minute. After returning from his call, he returned the cash to me and said he would follow up with me, but that something had come up. He left in a rush.

As I pulled into the shopping mall, I parked, got out of my car, and then took my time putting on my coat. I walked toward the shopping mall. As I was walking to the door, I could see the vehicle stop and two passengers getting out of the car. As one of the men got out, his coat jacket got caught. I could then see, in the reflection of the door, that he had a shoulder holster. My heart skipped a beat. What the fuck had I gotten myself into?

My phone rang. It was the FBI agent.

"Derek. I need you to buy something as soon as you can. Then head into the main part of the shopping mall. Get as far to the opposite end of the mall as you can. I'll then text you which exit to take. We are going to set off the fire alarm. Don't run, just try to duck out unnoticeably."

"Okay. Are you in here?" I asked.

"Yes."

I made my way to the opposite end of the mall, trying to seem normal. I stopped here and there to look at something in a store window. Then I got the text. It read, "Alarm going off in 30 seconds. Stay right there and take the exit to your left. Your car will be right there when you walk out. It's running. Just jump in it and go. I'll call you once we know it's clear."

As she said, the fire alarm went off. I hid behind the shopping mall directory. Then as everything got extremely crowded, I bent down and rushed to the exit. Sure enough, my car was there. I jumped in and took off.

When the agent finally called me, the plan had changed. I was no longer to head to meet them or to return to the airport. My new directive was to head straight to the executive airport where they arranged to get me back to California. It would be a long flight back home.

Once I landed, I met with the FBI agents the next day. They assured me they were looking into the men who had been following me but confirmed they were not law enforcement. We all agreed that I would stick to the Kevin Johnson investigation and work to wrap it up.

During this time, Kevin and I were scheduled to fly to New Haven to finish paying former Mayor Toni Harp. We still owed her a remaining balance for getting us the contract before she was defeated for reelection. On her last day as mayor, she pushed our contract through and signed it. No city hall meeting, no vote, no problem. In the coming weeks, we were also scheduled to fly to Los Angeles to follow up with our deal with Mayor Eric Garcetti. The FBI told me to send Kevin an email to confirm the trips before we booked the flights.

Are you free later? Kevin wrote in an email. *There are a few concerns that have come up and I need to talk to you about them in person. I'll reach out later and see if you're free.* He also told me that the trip to New Haven would be cancelled.

It would be days until I heard back from Kevin. He finally reached out and asked me to come over to his house in the next hour. I told him I was on my way back from San Francisco and would be there in about two hours. I immediately called Special Agent Bills to let her know.

She instructed me to head downtown to Sacramento and meet an agent at a hotel not far from Kevin's house in East Sacramento. When I got there, I called the agent and got the room number. Once I got inside, I was startled when I saw how many agents were in the room. There was a total of 11.

"What's going on?" I asked Special Agent Bills.

"Nothing. I just wanted you to feel safe, given that our last operation didn't go as planned," she said.

"Noooo . . . What's going on?"

"Derek, I am just making sure we have you covered. It's for safety."

"Do you think Kevin was connected to what happened?" I asked.

"We don't know yet, but we are looking into it. But we need to get you some equipment and get you on your way. We can talk about this later," she told me.

Then I was issued a cell phone and a debit card. The FBI no longer depended on wires/bugs, due to people being able to detect and find those more easily. This FBI cell phone was by far one of the best devices I have used throughout all the investigations I have participated in. It is a regular smartphone but with a special app. The app appeared to be a game; however, once I pressed a few buttons in the right sequence, it would open the real function.

The app was a secret video chat. I could turn it on and then exit out of it, back to the video game. The video game really worked; however, once activated, the phone would stream in live video and audio that it was capturing via the smartphone camera and microphone. This allowed the agents to hear and see what was going on in live time and record evidence. More important, it avoided detection. These days, everyone who has watched a spy movie or a police show knows they can buy a wire detector online for 50 bucks and scan their home, business, or car to detect and find wires. The FBI had long since moved on.

It was the same with the debit card. I had bank debit cards and gift certificate cards to name brand stores which the FBI had built recording devices out of. I would have to press and hold down on the card for a certain amount of time for the card to become active. Once I activated it, the card would record for up to two hours.

I took my devices and headed to Kevin's. Once I pulled up to his house, I could see that everything was completely pitch-black. I got out of my car and walked up to his door to knock on it. No one answered. I had somehow arrived before him. I called him to see where he was. He did not pick up, but he immediately texted me to let me know he would be there in a few minutes. Butterflies were starting to fly around in my stomach.

I went back to my car, got in, and turned it on. Doing my best to try to not look obvious, I started bobbing my head to appear that I was dancing in my car and singing. However, I was not singing lyrics, I was giving the agents an update to let them know what was going on.

Kevin's house was one of the rare houses in East Sacramento that had a back alley with a garage. Within a few minutes, I saw a light turn on in the house. Then Kevin was at the front door waving me to come on in.

As I got out of the car, I said, "Hey," and started walking to the house. Kevin walked in and did not wait for me.

"Are you okay? Everything good?" Kevin asked me. "Just want to make sure you're good."

"Yeah," I replied. "So, we're no longer going to New Haven. What's that about?"

"I haven't talked to Toni in a couple of months," Kevin said.

The FBI had been tracking all his phone records, so I knew Kevin had talked to Toni just days before. I was getting worried that Kevin had been tipped off to the investigation.

"What about Garcetti?" I asked.

"I don't know what you're talking about," Kevin said.

I showed him the email he had sent me just a few days before about Garcetti having questions.

About this time, the FBI texted me to drop the subject—something was up.

"Why don't you let me drive this conversation?" Kevin then said. "Let's talk about other people, about other stuff."

Later I found out that someone else was in the house. The other person was not moving, apparently just listening. I think what Kevin was trying to do was to get me to say something illegal to convince him I was not an informant.

Finally, he asked me, "How much did you give Harp for the contract?"

I told him I gave her $15,000 to land the contract. I could see his entire body suddenly relax at that point.

"I'm sorry," Kevin said. "We're both off tonight."

After that, we had a little small talk before jumping back into business. We talked about the restaurant, a soon-to-be pizza shop, and Black Capital, an investment company. However, I knew I had to steer the conversation back to the list of dirty politicians and who would be next.

I asked Kevin, "Who else is next? We need to get a few more to sell the company."

Kevin said he wanted to circle back to Stockton. Within minutes, he got Daniel Lopez on the phone from the City of Stockton and explained that we needed a contract there. This was great for the FBI because the FBI had the conversation recorded from Kevin's phone. They had been tapping Kevin's phone for years, which at times proved difficult because he was constantly changing numbers and phones.

Then an FBI agent texted me on my personal phone, asking me to take out my other phone because they were having trouble hearing us, due to it being in my pocket. The second phone was an FBI phone. This cell phone had an app that used the calling feature to receive live video and audio. I took out the FBI phone.

"When did you get another phone?" Kevin said.

"I've always had two phones," I said. "It's for work."

"Oh, let me see that," he said.

Shit, I was thinking. I hoped he would not ask to hold on to it and give it back later, or run through every app with me, or ask to turn it off. This was all possible. I've been in these types of meetings before, when Kevin would actually stop everything and ask the person who caused him suspicion to turn over their phone or ask them if there were okay to be searched. He was no fool—I knew he could open the app and at least notice something was fishy. However, I played it cool. I shrugged and handed him the phone.

He looked at me awkwardly and then started getting nervous again.

"I'm getting tired," he said. "Let's call it a night."

He walked me to the car.

"Are you okay?" he asked me, probably for the fifth or sixth time that night. "Do you need anything? If anyone is messing with you, bothering you, I got you covered. It doesn't matter who they are or what level they are. I got you."

"No," I said, "I'm good."

"What I'm doing is unique," Kevin said. "I appreciate you and I hope you appreciate me and that we are loyal to each other. I love you."

"Love you too, man," I said, thankful to be out of there.

I found out later that the FBI agents monitoring our conversation had moved their position points during the meeting. Cars cannot just park on the street in Kevin's neighborhood, a wealthy area where lots of politicians live. Someone would get suspicious and call the police. So, the FBI agents would swap out the cars every few minutes to avoid suspicion.

When Kevin started talking suspiciously to me, the agents had moved within 200 feet of his house, in case they needed to respond quickly. Luckily, it never came to that. The FBI asked me to set up another meeting, with nothing controversial on the agenda. So, we had a routine meeting about Black Capital.

I was supportive of everything Kevin was saying about the company. He told me the company needed $25,000 for travel and other expenses.

"Okay, I'll do a no-interest loan," I told Kevin. He loved that.

After I left the meeting and was headed to meet with the FBI, Kevin called me.

"I just talked to Mayor Harp," Kevin said. "She's good. We do not have to finish paying her. No need for the trip to New Haven."

"Cool," I said.

I was not sure exactly what was going on, but something was definitely off with Kevin Johnson.

CHAPTER NINETEEN
STOCKTON

During that meeting, which would be one of my last meetings with Kevin at his home, Kevin introduced some more politicians from the list into the mix.

"Okay. I'm thinking I can circle back with Mayor Tubbs and Daniel over in Stockton. That cool?" Kevin asked.

"Yeah," I replied.

Kevin then took out his phone and started texting them. Within minutes, Daniel Lopez, who served as the senior advisor for Mayor Michael Tubbs of Stockton, and Mayor Tubbs, called Kevin.

"Mayor Johnson, how's it going?" they asked.

"I'm good, Mayor. How are you doing? How are things going in Stockton?" Kevin replied.

"Everything is all good. We've been busy," said Tubbs.

"Mayor Tubbs is running his new campaign. We just had presidential candidate Bloomberg in the house, crime is down, and the city is growing. So, no complaints," Daniel added.

"That's awesome. Look, I wanted to circle back with you regarding the government tech company that we discussed before," Kevin said.

"Yeah, yeah, yeah. How can we help?" they asked.

"Look, we need another contract with a city immediately. We can do something for parking, tech, collections, or anything. We just need you to get it to us," Kevin proposed.

"No problem, Mayor," said Tubbs.

"And then, of course, like we discussed last time, we can come through for your campaign," Kevin said.

"Well, the mayor is running a campaign right now," Daniel replied.

"Great. We will support him and any initiatives that need funding or money. We just need this to happen ASAP. Generally, I would not say over the phone quid pro quo, but I'm in a rush! So, I am saying quid pro quo. What do you need to get this done?" asked Kevin. It was almost like Kevin was working for the feds instead of me!

"Okay. Well, send me over the list of services that you can perform. Then we will find a fit," Daniel said.

"Great. Derek will get it to you in the next day," Kevin said.

In my mind, I was thinking, *Oh, no!* I was really looking forward to this case being wrapped up. In recent months, some things had felt off. I was no longer happy. At some points, as I was starting to build back doors and holes, I would question myself on my retaliation methods. Outside of that, I had been constantly feeling like I had been put in uncomfortable positions, and that I was still being watched by the bad guys. Now this idiot was introducing more elected officials to this investigation and we were going to have to pursue them.

I could only imagine what all the FBI agents were thinking when they heard this conversation. The teams were sitting in their cars outside the house, within a minute from the location.

Nonetheless, after the meeting, I met up with the FBI agents and we had our quick debrief and went home. We all figured we would just continue to go down the path of wrapping up the case with no new targets.

Two days later, the text I had been dreading came. It was from one of the FBI special agents.

"Hey, did you send that email to Stockton?" it said.

Damn, I was thinking. *Washington must want us to pursue it.*

"Not yet. I'll send it now."

I then opened my phone, went into my email, and clicked compose. I started the email to Daniel by referencing the call Daniel had with Kevin within the past few days, and then I went into the services that the company provided. The reason I did this was to have Daniel confirm that it was him who was speaking with the mayor and communicating with us to get a contract. Although everything was recorded on FBI devices, it is always nice to have a little extra written evidence. By this time though, everyone was being taped and recorded.

Almost as soon as I pressed send, I received a response from Daniel. He thanked me for sending this over and told me they would follow up.

Days later, I met with everyone on the FBI team. It was game time. Time to start getting all the paperwork together to get the warrants, and, more importantly, time to go kick down some doors. During our meeting, Stockton popped up again.

"Have you heard anything back from Stockton?" one of the agents asked.

"No, not yet. Want me to send a text?" I replied.

"Yeah."

Within minutes, Daniel Lopez called me. *Oh crap*. We were not prepared to take the call at that time, so I ignored it and texted him that I would call right back. One of the agents and I then stepped out and I called him back.

"Hey, Daniel. How's it going?"

"Good, man. How are you doing?"

"I'm doing good. Sorry I couldn't pick up; I was just wrapping up another call."

"No worries."

"So, what's up?"

"Nothing. I just wanted to let you know that I got your text and the mayor and I are working on getting a date finalized for this week or early next week."

"Okay, cool," I said.

"One little problem, though. The email you sent me following up about the campaign is a big no-no. We don't want to get caught up or anything. So, don't email me anything referencing that," he said.

"Of course. My bad, man."

"No worries. We are still going to meet and everything. Just wanted to tell you that. I double-checked about the day and time, and the mayor's scheduler said it's already in the works," he said.

"Oh. Okay. Great. Thanks, Daniel," I replied.

We then stayed on the line for a few more minutes talking about life, the San Francisco 49ers going to the Super Bowl, and our weekend plans. I wrapped up the call, and the agent and I went back in to update the team.

Something that caught our attention was that Daniel had stated on the call that a meeting was "already in the works." This piqued our curiosity. Had Kevin reached out to Mayor Tubbs directly to schedule something? We did not know, but we would surely find out.

Daniel and Mayor Tubbs got back to me a few days later. We had set a meeting for Thursday, February 6, 2020. Boy, was that pushing it. The FBI had already made plans to go kick down some doors and arrest people by then. However, why not add one more corrupt politician? It would just be a cherry on top, although a small cherry, as Stockton was not exactly Los Angeles.

I met with Mayor Tubbs and Daniel Lopez on February 6, 2020, at the city hall in Stockton. Per usual, I met up with the FBI agents before the meeting to get equipped, and then we all headed to city hall. It took less than five minutes to get up the stairs and into the meeting with the mayor.

Everything had already been arranged, so it was now just time to pick a service. The mayor, his team, and I discussed all the services that the company I was pretending to be part of offered. He agreed to put out an RFP and give the company a contract to build a "scholars app," and then to make sure they could amend and create a special "parking enforcement" contract for us, too. The conversation soon turned to the money.

"I still need to raise about $35,000 dollars within the next ten days," said Mayor Tubbs.

"Okay. I think I can do about $25,000 of that. Let me get back to Mayor Johnson, and I'll have him connect with you to finalize something," I said.

"All right, cool," Tubbs replied.

"Before I go, let's grab a quick picture," I said.

"Of course!"

Little did they know, outside city hall in a silver van were several FBI agents, listening live. I could almost hear them singing: "And another . . . and another . . . and another one bites the dust."

When I returned to my car outside city hall, Special Agent Austin Harper and Special Agent Russ texted me. They informed me to follow them down the road, where we could park and they could collect their devices.

Once we reached the location, we got out of the car, and went over the meeting. Not bad. It had been a success. They said that Agent Bills wanted us to give her a call right after.

"Great job, Derek. Let's get together on Monday. We heard back from headquarters. There are some more mayors on the list that we need to pursue."

No way, I was thinking. *That was not part of the plan.*

"I thought we were done," I replied.

"No, remember we talked about wrapping up the list?"

"Noooo . . ."

"Derek, here you go again, forgetting what we talked about. This is the same thing that happened about your case getting dismissed."

I was immediately infuriated. How dare she insult my intelligence. *What a slap in the face,* I thought. But I knew I had to go along with it.

"That's right. Okay, just let me know Sunday what time to come in on Monday and we can get together and figure out the plan."

"Perfect. Talk soon," she said.

CHAPTER TWENTY
VENTURE CAPITAL

Unbeknownst to Kevin, Black Capital would be his last venture. As he had been out of office for a few years with no big wins, Kevin was looking to do something noticeable. Over time, Kevin and I had jumped in and out of several ventures, and we were always bouncing ideas off each other.

One person who Kevin could never figure out was Troy Carter, best known as the manager of Lady Gaga—yes, the well-known artist, actor, and activist. In addition, Troy managed rapper Eve. He opened his own production company, a venture capital (VC) firm, and more. Kevin was in awe of him. How could this guy, who was much younger, be worth more than him? Troy had a net worth of about $50 million at that time, while Kevin had a net worth of about $15 million.

This vision of Troy having his own VC firm or fund started in March 2016. We invited Troy to attend one of the events at IndiviZible, a group of African Americans in Sacramento who meet to help the greater community, to speak about "how he did it." Troy was authentic, inspirational, and legit—all the things Kevin did not add up to.

Later, Kevin told me he wanted to get more involved with techs, startups, and venture capital. One night when we were at our office, located at the 40-acre complex in the Oak Park district of Sacramento, Troy was on Kevin's mind again.

"Hey, D, we gotta try to get some investing firm put together, like a VC," Kevin said.

I had learned that VC was a venture capital form of private investors, a type of financing that investors provide to startup companies. Generally, the startup would have to have early signs of success or have groundbreaking technology. Typically, a VC would raise about $100 million from investors and then use those funds to invest in startups. The VC would take a portion of the money raised and get money from the companies it invested in.

"What do you mean?" I asked, wanting to get a better understanding of which type of VC he was thinking about.

"Troy is running around out here investing in companies left and right. He is making money while he is sleeping. How can we do that?"

"Well, I am sure that it is one hell of a process to start a venture capital firm and to become compliant with the US Securities and Exchange Commission and all. I can look into it, if you like?"

"I want to do something big. Like, let's make a big minority fund. Get all the minorities to give us money and then we go out and invest it in startups and techs."

"Well, there are already companies that do something like that. There's this crowdsourcing platform that allows both accredited and nonaccredited investors to invest online on its platform in startups that it likes. Do you want me to look at it?" I asked.

"Well, what's the name?" he urged.

I told him the name of the crowdsourcing platform, SeedInvest.

"Well, hold off for now," he said.

Weeks later, I received a random text from Kevin. He was excited. He told me I should join him in New York because he was having a potential partnership meeting with SeedInvest, the company I had just told him about. In my mind, I was thinking, *such a sneaky little bastard*. However, I was also intrigued and told him to fill me in. He had been in conversation with Ryan Feit, the CEO and cofounder of SeedInvest, for a few weeks, and they had been going back and forth on working together to create a "black fund." Things were getting close to being finalized and now it was time to go out there and make it final.

After months of hard work and direction from the FBI, we were at the point where we had a company name, a plan, and an agreement to partner with the world's largest crowdsourcing online investment platform. The potential was . . . tens of millions of dollars.

The plan was to initially raise $20 million: $10 million from unaccredited investors and $10 million from accredited investors. However, Kevin's plan went one step further. Kevin wanted me to go out and find the startups. Then I would set up meetings with Kevin and the startups to work out an agreement. They would have to pay to play. If they paid Kevin, then he would send them back to me and have me prep them to make them investment worthy, and then send them through the due diligence process with the partner company. Thankfully, at this point, the FBI was already on board and capturing everything on audio and video.

It was illegal for a fund to defraud investors by telling them it would put startups through due diligence and only fund a portion of the startups that passed when, in fact, the fund was only going to give money to companies that paid the fund to sign off on them.

Kevin then put together a group of professionals who would represent Black Capital. I would be sitting at the table with Kevin Johnson and several others, who I will not name because they are good people and had no clue as to what Kevin's true plans were. However, everybody at the table was carefully chosen. One man held a special license called the Series 7 broker's license. Kevin knew to approach him on the topic with the cover story of wanting to do business with him because he was African American. It was a strategic business move, in case Kevin had trouble passing all three tests and exams to get the proper licenses himself.

The Series 7 license is an essential license for a broker, and the exam is quite challenging. The Series 7 exam authorizes the holder to sell all types of securities and related products, except for commodities, insurance products, and futures. Stockbrokers need to pass the Series 7 exam to obtain a license to trade. The Series 7 exam focuses on investment risk, taxation, equity and debt instruments, packaged securities, options, retirement plans, and interactions with clients.

There came a point where the question arrived from the government: Did SeedInvest know what was going on? Did it know what Kevin's plan was? Why would a company take a chance with someone who had undergone many criminal investigations? Did SeedInvest not care? It appeared that the company was only interested in money, however, we would put this to test.

The plan was to send an anonymous email to the executives at SeedInvest, informing them of potential risk and liabilities to come if they continued with one of their partnerships, and see how they responded. However, after several weeks of back-and-forth communications, SeedInvest would continue to do business with Black Capital. This brought up many questions. What else was the company doing? After all, SeedInvest had a fiduciary duty to its shareholders. However, that would be another team at another office to follow up on.

Everything Kevin did was always strategic. He always knew who he could do business with and what motivated them. Life and business were both a chess game for Kevin.

As the Kevin Johnson case would start to wrap up, I would try my best to postpone, delay, and slow the progress of Black Capital, to spare these good people and the crowdsourcing company their good names and reputations. Little did they know what was coming around the corner.

CHAPTER TWENTY-ONE

THE PRESIDENTIAL ELECTION

T oward the end of 2019, I was asked to help investigate a 2020 presidential candidate. I knew that this was top level. There would be no discussion of this via text, email, or phone due to the sensitivity. Little did I know that my openness to do this would lead to more candidates down the road.

The first candidate I had been asked to investigate was being pursued because of an alleged tip that had been received along with an audiotape. However, what I found weird was that the source was unknown. At first I was skeptical, because this was the first time I had been asked to go after presidential candidate, and it was the first time the FBI didn't provide me with any information regarding the source(s) and credibility of the allegations. Lastly, there was no paperwork regarding the investigation. Again, this was completely inconsistent with all the practices that were followed with the prior investigations into other targets.

All I was told was that the candidate needed money to keep the campaign going and was starting to bend the line, making unethical commitments and possibly breaching campaign finance laws. The FBI got me a meeting. The agents had created a whole new alias for me for this job. Driver's license, taxes, Social Security number, birth certificate, you name it. Hell, I was not even from California. We would use a fake company as my cover, offering campaign cash in exchange for the promise of leading the way to get federal laws changed, or to get appointments or pardons. In fact, I was instructed to lead with anything the candidate seemed most comfortable with. Now, this did not seem above board. This sounded like entrapment, and I did not like it.

The meeting was to take place after hours at the candidate's campaign office. As usual, I met with the FBI agents before going to the meeting and was issued the cell phone recorder and the debit card. When I arrived, there were still people working. I was surprised, because it was late. Nonetheless, I checked in with one of the candidate's team members and was asked to take a seat. Within a few minutes, the candidate appeared, looking tired and stressed.

"Hi, Mr. Williams, nice to meet you," the candidate said, knowing only my undercover name.

"Thanks. Nice to meet you too," I replied.

We then went into an office and made small talk. The candidate shared some goals and dreams with me, as I did in return. I had been prepped about this person for two weeks at this point. I knew what to say to gain the candidate's interest, and I knew the things the candidate was passionate about.

After about 20 minutes, we finally arrived at the topic we were both only truly interested in. What does the candidate need and what do I need? The candidate was telling me they needed to raise some serious funds and was now exploring all options. And, more importantly, that the people who were showing up and backing the candidate would surely not be forgotten. I took the lead at that moment. I started making my pitch for government services, a potential pardon for a friend, and other needs. The candidate agreed. Then a staffer knocked and came in.

There was a development in information that had just come in regarding one of the candidates they could use in their favor. The

THE MIGHTY HAVE FALLEN

candidate asked if we could follow up with each other in the next day or two, because I had shared that I would be in town for a few days.

"Of course," I said.

As I was walking out, the candidate handed me a glossy folder in the most awkward way, holding it only by the corner tip. The candidate waited until I grabbed it and then said, "Wait. Wrong one," and took it back, in the same awkward way. I remember thinking, *how strange*, as the candidate grabbed the folder from me, then replaced it with a completely different item. It was an envelope which could not have been mistaken for the item they had given me originally. It was enclosed with some of the candidate's campaign material and more information about the candidate.

After the meeting, I drove back to our rendezvous spot to meet with the agents. Apparently, they had also noticed the weird folder exchange. However, the reason would not become known to us until later.

I stayed in town for a few days and received a follow-up call from the candidate. The candidate liked what was discussed, however, would be traveling and asked if we could meet in two weeks when the candidate thought they would be visiting the town they believed I lived in. I agreed.

A few days later, I received a call from one of the FBI agents. Apparently, my fingerprints had just been run through a national law enforcement system and the FBI had been alerted. The agent believed that it was the candidate, who had gotten my fingerprints from the folder. The investigation into this candidate was now over. The candidate knew, or was about to find out, my true identity.

Thankfully, the FBI received authorization to monitor the candidate's communication devices. Once confirmed that it was the candidate who had run my prints, the FBI coordinated with the US Attorney's Office and went to speak with the candidate. The FBI did not tell me what exactly happened, but what they did share was that the candidate would be ending their campaign.

Later, one of the agents shared with me that I had been doing a great job and my work had led to a presidential candidate having to step down and work with the US Department of Justice. However, I did not feel good about it. I knew we were no longer running true investigations, but being led and directed by the leadership and outsiders for political reasons.

I was being told that the Washington office was pleased with my progress and commitment to the FBI. It just so happened the FBI had received another report regarding another presidential candidate. *Bullshit*, I thought. Same political party and same type of weird background, missing many details. I then decided to share this with one of my private attorneys, since the Bureau refused to let me discuss the investigation with my counsel for my own case. It was not until then that I really became concerned. My attorney, who had worked on civil matters for me, brought up a troubling conspiracy theory.

He asked me if I remembered what happened in the 2016 presidential election with presidential nominee Hillary Clinton. I told him I vaguely remembered. He reminded me that days before it was time to vote, the director of the FBI had sent a letter regarding Hillary Clinton, saying the FBI was going to be looking into new emails that had just been found relating to the investigation. He said it had cost her the presidential race.[1]

My attorney had a theory that perhaps this could be a new way of the FBI trying to interfere with the presidential election. Dare I tell him we had been funding numerous Republican campaigns, in which these candidates won office, which then resulted in us stopping our alleged investigations? Was I being used for some crazy plot? Would I eventually be thrown under the bus? *Over my dead body*, I thought. And thankfully, I'd been taking measures to cover my ass just in case.

To keep myself balance, I also had to remind myself that the people who I had been meeting with—from mayors, to members of Congress, and others—were not clean people. That was fact. But I had come to realize the saying: If you put a cop behind someone to tail them, after long enough, they will find a reason to pull them over.

Nonetheless, I once again in a conversation with Special Agent

Rebekah Bills, once again requesting I meet with yet another presidential candidate.

I DECIDED I needed to challenge this. I wanted to know who the source was, and how exactly we were investigating yet another presidential candidate of the same party. I was being asked to mislead and not involve my attorney or pre-trial court appointed supervisor Tai, and send communication via text/email asking if I could stay longer in cities/trips paid for by the FBI for personal time. In fact, I was staying on longer trips "off the books" to investigate some other presidential candidates among other politicians. My concern was, if this were legit, why was SA Bills not including others from the Bureau in this? More importantly, why was I being asked to send communications to them and others stating my extended stay would be for personal reasons? It reminded me of the days Kevin would have me correspond at his direction to cover his own ass. I wasn't about to fall into this predicament again. I wanted to be assured that this was not a targeted investigation.

"Something seems off with this, Rebekah. What's going on?" I asked.

"Derek, I just got the file. It seemed credible and I am just following up on it," said Agent Bills.

"Can I see the report that came in from the source? Is it credible?" You can imagine my concern.

"I can't share that with you."

"Why not? I have always been able to review the reports and files prior to all the other investigations, but not this one?"

She seemed frustrated by my questioning. But also, she seemed nervous.

"Derek, I don't even think there is a file. This is above my head, and I was just assigned it," she said.

There it was. Again. Another lie. She had just said that she had reviewed the file.

"I think I can connect you with the source, though. Let me get approval and then I will get back to you, okay?" she offered.

A day later, Agent Bills called and told me she had been able to get approval and was going to set up a meeting so that we could get more information from the "source." It seemed sketched to me. However, I figured I would invest a little into this to confirm.

Special Agent Bills wanted to meet out in Loomis, California, close to where she resided. This was a first, but not uncommon. Generally, we had always met at the office or somewhere around the office, such as a coffee shop, bank, or park. However, she wanted me to meet her out by her residence and in the middle of nowhere. I wasn't too suspicious, though, because we had already far passed the rules of handler and CHS. The Department of Justice had strong processes and procedures for when it came to how FBI agents could interact on a personal and professional level with confidential human sources. They were not allowed to divulge personal information or make promises regarding one's case. However, by this point, Special Agent Bills had already introduced me to some members of her family, including one of her kids, on several occasions and more.

Nonetheless, I agreed to meet up the next day. However, I figured it was best to reach out to an associate of mine who had a knack for these type of things to tail the alleged source after the meeting. My suspicions were that strong. How could a source be meeting with us in the middle of the week, when they were supposed to be very close to a presidential candidate in the middle of their campaign? It just didn't add up. So, I followed my gut.

My associate arrived an hour early before our meeting. He set up shop about a quarter mile away, and launched his drone upon receiving my signal. I would text him when I was pulling up. He was to only get a visual on the vehicle that arrived, or was present upon my arrival. I knew Agent Bills would be driving either her work vehicle, a tan Ford Fusion, or her personal vehicle, a white Honda civic. So, that meant whichever other car was there belonged to the source. His job was to identify the vehicle and tail it upon leaving. I would tell Agent Bills I wanted to stay behind to talk to her about some other developments on another case.

When I got into the car, I could tell right off the bat that this guy was in no way associated with a campaign. He was muscle. However, I figured I would play along with it. After quick introductions, we got right into the key question. Why did he contact the FBI regarding the candidate he was working for, and why was he certain there was corruption? As he started to go into his answer, I interrupted him and asked a question he should have known the answer to:

"Is Chris still running all the canvassers over there? I actually used to work with him a few years ago when he was on Steinberg's campaign."

Now, I did not have any clue who Chris was nor did I work for Steinberg's campaign, but I figured this was a good question to throw him off his game and make him think on his feet. However, he quickly looked at Agent Bills, and she looked at me.

"Yeah. I think so. Things have been so hectic lately, and our team has just been growing in size. Just this week, we've added about 30 people," the source said.

Yep. Just as I had figured. He had no clue as to who Chris was, because it was a made-up name. This guy was bogus. Furthermore, if they were running out of money and needed funds, why would they be hiring such large groups of people? It just didn't add up. I did my best to engage in the rest of the conversation and seem sold on him being who he claimed and wanting to move forward to capture the corruption. As planned, I asked Rebekah if I could stay behind to talk to her regarding another case. The source shook my hand and said he wasn't sure if he would be seeing me again, as he was planning to submit his resignation soon.

Sure . . . I thought.

Nonetheless, the source got into his vehicle and took off. My mind was beginning to wonder. Did my associate have time to land his drone and tail the source without losing him? How long should I stay to make it seem like I genuinely had some new information to discuss? Ten minutes, I decided.

After leaving Rebekah, I pulled out my other phone and called my associate. I knew I had to continue taking additional safety measures. I was constantly buying new burner phones every week to communicate with my counsel and other sources. My associate had told me he was tailing the source and that they were just exiting the freeway next to Top Golf. *Interesting*, I thought. Not two minutes later, the "source" was pulling into the Roseville FBI office and entering past the security gate, meaning they had credentials. Meaning, they were not a source. They were an employee of the FBI.

This was beyond wild. What was I to do? My first thought was to contact the DOJ Office of the Inspector General. This was the office that monitored the FBI and served as an internal affairs organization for corruption. However, I had to consider . . . what if this blew up in my face? What if they contacted the FBI and alerted them? I did not want to take the risk. I figured it would be best to continue moving forward and collecting what I could to bring this matter to light in the end.

As time would progress, I was assigned to help investigate several other politicians. However, Agent Bills started to grow suspicious, and then figured out I had been on to her for some time and that she was in some trouble.

CHAPTER TWENTY-TWO
A CHANGING RELATIONSHIP

My relationship with the Department of Justice, specifically the US Attorney's Office, had changed quickly. Ever since the beginning, Assistant United States Attorney Todd Pickles asked me to take a leap of faith with him. To trust him, the Bureau, and the Department of Justice. To let go of my past ways and commit to a new way to help fight for justice. He was a very genuine, trustworthy, and honest man. He told me they had to believe I wanted to be part of the team and that I would do as directed by the agents, to ensure the integrity of the investigations that would come. He said, "You have to be honest with us. Because we are going to be honest with you. I give you my word that we will not do anything intentionally to mislead or put you in danger. You can trust the agents, and my office. We are built on trust and integrity. The minute that anyone crosses those lines, this will fall apart." He asked me to commit, and I saw no reason not to.

A couple weeks into the investigation, I started to meet some of the actual bosses. Also, during this time, Assistant United States Attorney Todd Pickles notified us that he was leaving the US Attorney's Office and taking a job at a private law firm. My case was transferred to Matthew Yelovich, who would be in charge for several months until he, too, ultimately notified us that he was leaving, as well. My case was then again transferred to another assistant United States attorney. Her name was Amy Hitchcock. She was a sharp attorney who had been with the US Attorney's Office for over 12 years.

Before my indictment in 2018, I had not had much personal experience with this office; however, I did have a few friends who had worked for various US Attorney's Offices throughout the US. On top of that, my only impressions about the office and the US attorneys had been formed from the TV show, *Billions*, which starred a US attorney—good old Chuck Rhoades, portrayed by Paul Giamatti. That fierce, ass-kicking US attorney laid down the law.

I met the real-life equivalent of the show's main character, and his name was AUSA Michael Anderson. He was the chief of the White-Collar Crime Unit. My assessment of AUSA Anderson when we met at the initial meeting was that he was a true advocate for justice. He had gone to the UCLA School of Law and done quite well there. He then took the Bar and was admitted in 2005. He had mostly been kicking butt and climbing the ladder since then.

I did a lot of research about this office, its statistics, and its process. I was surprised to learn that the attorneys prosecute and win over 90 percent of their cases![1] That was surprising, as I was more familiar with the state court statistics, where the successful cases would be in the high sixtieth percentile, depending on which state you were being prosecuted in. Nonetheless, this office meant business, and I could tell it only brought cases it knew the attorneys could win. I would later find out why. The "why" is because the other agencies located under the US Department of Justice work so hard and long to get consistent information, confirmation, and evidence of a crime before prosecuting it.

I remember I would go out for an operation and know I was capturing good evidence. Then I would hear back that it was good, but they needed more! I would lose my mind.

On one of the operations, the subject said, "Yeah, we need a quid pro quo, how much do you need to get us this contract?"

I said to myself, "Boom! Done!"

Then I would hear back, "Ehh. It's okay. But we need more."

My mind would explode. "What?! More? I don't know how much more I can do."

However, this was just the way the US Attorney's Office wanted to build an airtight case—and build an airtight case, it did.

Unfortunately, very early on, Special Agent Rebekah Bills began not only lying to me, but misleading me. First it was about my friends and the company having any liability for being used as a front for the FBI. From there, it only expanded. It ranged from having me commit and break laws without signing or doing the proper paperwork, to signing and transmitting information which was not correct. However, the last straw was Agent Bills lying about having my case dismissed. That is what caused me to make sure all the cases that she in particular was working on would possibly not be prosecuted.

CHAPTER TWENTY-THREE
GRAND JURIES

T hroughout my time working for the FBI, as investigations were ending, we knew we would need to prepare for the legal battles ahead, or at least help the US Attorney's Office prepare. Throughout most of the cases I was involved in, we had strong evidence. Then there were some cases where we got acknowledgment and quid pro quos, however, we did not follow through on them.

Generally, upon an investigation wrapping up and heading for prosecution, the FBI and the US Attorney's Office wanted to first obtain a search and seizure warrant. This was because although it had recordings, videos, and other evidence, nothing was better than having the actual physical evidence from the suspect in the case. The FBI was granted permission to monitor mayors' cell phones, other phones, emails, and accounts.

Often, politicians will try to say they were unaware of certain activity, that it was a staffer of theirs. That is because it is not uncommon for politicians, chiefs of staff, or aides to communicate on behalf of their leaders. This would make a jury think twice about a conviction. That is why the government likes to confiscate the politicians' actual personal devices, which only they have access to. Then, it is more of the hand-in-the-cookie-jar argument. It's much easier to prove to a jury that it was the suspect's personal phone, that it was them sending specific text messages, making those calls, or sending emails from that mobile device, computer, or tablet.

With other cases, the government wanted to simply subpoena records and get authorization to monitor targets' cell phones, emails, and more. There was such damning evidence from their devices that the government officials wanted to make sure they were able to collect those pieces of evidence before the devices were destroyed or the politicians could alter them.

After the evidence was collected through the subpoena request and search and seizure warrants, it was downloaded and inspected by the FBI team. The team would review and verify all emails, texts, calls, location information, and more to support the case the FBI would bring.

To bring a case, there would generally be a federal grand jury. As these people were US residents, the common process was that it would be alleged they violated a federal law. The reason is because each resident is guaranteed the right to a federal grand jury proceeding, where the case and the evidence will be presented to the grand jury to decide if any or all federal charges listed in a federal criminal complaint should move forward.

This is the suspect's legal right under the US Constitution, found under the Fifth Amendment, which specifies, *No person shall be held to answer for a capital, or otherwise infamous crime, unless on a presentment or indictment of a Grand Jury.*[1] In rare cases, the federal grand jury process also relates to any foreign nationals living inside the boundaries of the United States, in addition to those who might be at large or residing and in hiding abroad. People could be indicted in absentia.

A federal grand jury is made up of 16 to 23 panel members and is assembled after a federal investigation is begun by the US Attorney's

Office, or after a federal complaint is filed by the arresting agency. The process is secret and not administered by a judge or magistrate. Most suspects generally have no idea that this grand jury is even taking place. The grand juries are all confidential and sealed. Outside the grand jury, it is generally just the US attorney, FBI agents (those who the case belongs to or those who worked the case), and key witnesses who know what is happening. I fell under the key witness category, as I was a confidential human source and independent contractor.

When a federal complaint is brought to a grand jury, those making up the panel will hear evidence presented by the complainant. The complainant in the cases I worked was always an attorney from the US Attorney's Office or an assistant US attorney. They always lead these hearings. They would present the evidence to the grand jury, guiding them in deciding if a crime, or a number of crimes, had been committed by the accused, and whether there was enough cause to pursue that suspect for a future trial. The US attorney's job is to present a strong case with compelling evidence that will convince the grand jury to hand down an indictment.

Now, it is important to remember that the grand jury process is not a trial. The objective of this is to present the case to the grand jury to show enough cause that there should be an indictment handed down so that a trial can take place. This practice is extended under the Federal Rules of Criminal Procedure, when a federal grand jury by a simple majority of its members agrees to bring forward an indictment.

Unlike a regular trial jury, a decision by a grand jury does not have to be unanimous. If the majority's decision is in the affirmative to the allegations of the complaint, once coming to that determination, demonstrating a more than likely probability that the charges have merit based on the presented evidence, the panel returns what is known as a "true bill." If the result of the majority's opinion is that the presented facts are not believable or strong enough, and they will most likely not return a conviction at trial, the panel will presumably return what is called a "no bill," ending the current case.

However, because a grand jury hearing does not follow the same rules of evidence as a regular trial, a suspect's right to their own defense is principally limited. The US attorney who lays out all the charges is not compelled to inform the grand jury of evidence that might be favorable for the accused, and the defendant is not represented by counsel during the proceedings. This basically gives the leading advocates for the prosecution free rein, and allows them complete discretion for permitting the panel to hear only the facts and scenarios they want them to recognize.

Typically, when the United States Attorneys Office has an agent or their source testify at these grand juries, that is all that is truly needed to secure the indictment. Being that, I was working directly with the mayor, member of Congress, elected official, and government staff involved. At other times, I would pose as a local business owner, or I would buy in to one of the companies they were already illegally doing business with. Occasionally, I had to befriend some of the suspect's closest friends and family, and even at one time date one of their family members, to gain an "in" to the circle.

Nonetheless, when I would testify in front of the grand jury, I would answer basic questions. We would review video and audio evidence, and I would confirm what the members of the grand jury had just heard, and sometimes elaborate on it.

Because the Federal Rules of Evidence are not in force, a prosecutor can decide which evidence to present to the panel, ask questions that would be considered leading, and follow a line of questioning that would be deemed irrelevant if presented at a trial. If the accused is not yet in custody, they might not even know a hearing is going on. If an arrest has already taken place, the suspect is not allowed to present contrary evidence, or to tell their side of the story, and is not given access to the testimony of the prosecution until, if and when, a regular trial commences.

Additionally, because there is no defense counsel to act as an advocate for the accused, jurors can consider many arguments that would be objectionable in a regular trial. Some of these elements include evidence that might have been illegally, or obtained in addition to evidence that might be considered hearsay. Because federal grand jury members are not isolated, they might also improperly make their personal decisions based on media coverage of the case rumors and their own familiarity with the suspected crimes.

CHAPTER TWENTY-FOUR
THE FIGHT AGAINST CORRUPTION

During my time working for the FBI, there have been several takedowns, grand juries, and convictions. However, as of this writing, there have not been any trials. Of course, after the takedown happens and the suspect is taken into custody, they immediately plead "not guilty" and are bailed out of custody. This was the same for me. The reason this happens is not because the suspects (now defendants) truly believe they are not guilty. By doing this, it allows them better chances to get bail, obtain counsel, and prepare to see how solid of a case the US Attorney's Office has against them.

As I have mentioned throughout this book, the US Attorney's Office loves to have more than a solid case. Rarely do the attorneys build their cases on one piece of damning evidence. They continue to work the agents, confidential human sources, witnesses, and others involved in the case to capture additional and consistent evidence. This way, if an attorney can get the court to rule out one piece of evidence, the government still has a ton of other evidence to try the client, and most likely, win.

The data shows there were about 80,000 federal criminal cases brought by the government in 2018. Out of those cases, less than 1 percent were able to walk away with a "not guilty" verdict. Looking at that 1 percent, generally, the cases were not of the main defendant, but those who were charged as a co-conspirator or for a lesser crime. This shows you that the US Attorney's Office does a damn good job when it comes to preparing a case.

In the TV show *Law and Order,* prosecutors will generally offer the defendant a plea deal. This is when the government gives the defendant an option to admit their guilt. In exchange, the government will remove some of the charges. This will often result in the defendant having a lower sentence guideline. However, the government can also make recommendations.

What about for the few who try to keep the image of innocence and want to fight the charges? Well, it does not generally end well for them. When a guilty defendant continues to try to avoid their punishment, by not only refusing to recognize what they've done wrong and refusing to show remorse, but then deciding to continue the process that costs the taxpayers more money to try their cases, the courts, probation, and prosecutor generally throw the book at them.

In federal court, when someone pleads guilty or is found guilty, a full, detailed report is done on the case. An official of the court reviews the facts of the case, the person, and the family, including criminal history, work history, community efforts, and, more importantly, what steps have been taken since committing the crime to become a better person. If someone went to trial and lost, then that generally shows they are not remorseful. So, when it comes to sentencing guidelines, the highest guidelines are probably going to be recommended. Depending on the seriousness of the case, an upward departure might be recommended.

For example, in the case of Catherine Pugh, former mayor of Baltimore, she was initially indicted on 11 federal counts and faced close to 30 years if she were found guilty. However, the US Attorney's Office offered her a plea deal where she had to only accept and agree to being guilty to fewer than half of the charges. The government had a strong case—hand-in-the-cookie-jar evidence. However, the officials wanted Pugh to do the right thing, admit her guilt, and still have a chance at life. Pugh was sentenced to three years in prison, compared to the nearly 30 years she could have been sentenced to.

It will be interesting to see what Kevin Johnson does. This is a well-connected man. He has a lot of information and evidence about other crimes that have taken place, and the government wants to know all about them. For the cases we worked, I wonder if he will enter a proffer and cooperation agreement to help solve other crimes and wrap up investigations involving other politicians.

CHAPTER TWENTY-FIVE
IS YOUR LOCAL GOVERNMENT CORRUPT?

I am sure, by now, you are wondering how your local government falls into this. You are probably asking, "Is my mayor or member of Congress on that list?" or "Have my local politicians taken illegal bribes for contracts or unfairly defrauded the people and businesses to give a contract to a friend?"

I cannot share that information, however, because I would be putting investigations in jeopardy, and more importantly, I could be charged with obstruction of justice myself for ruining an ongoing investigation.

By assisting US Attorney's offices, IRS offices, other agencies, and, of course, FBI offices throughout the nation, I take pride in knowing I helped take down some corrupt politicians across the country. Though most will never know me, a few people will finally connect me to the guy who showed up out of nowhere and helped make their city a little better. Some of the government staff I met will soon know that it was me who helped take down the corruption in their city. However, most will never know my real identity, until maybe now.

I have come to realize another sad truth: Mayors and other politicians getting indicted for corruption is no longer news to law

THE MIGHTY HAVE FALLEN

enforcement agencies. Just in the past year, I worked many cases where there have been many mayors indicted and arrested, ranging from charges of bribery, extortion, fraud, and more. What has happened to America?

To give you courage, here is a summary of the cases pursued after hard work and investigations were completed in 2019. This list does not include every mayor or public official charged with corruption that year, and it certainly does not include any elected officials who are still under investigation. Remember, Kevin provided us with a list of over 40 politicians who have participated in illegal activity. I am sure that he'll try to use this as his "get out of jail free card."

DENNIS TYLER, FORMER MAYOR OF MUNCIE, INDIANA

Dennis Tyler was indicted in November 2019 for accepting illegal cash payments in return for awarding lucrative city contracts, including a charge of accepting a $5,000 bribe, according to the US Attorney's Office. He has pled not guilty and is expected to stand trial in August 2020. His mayoral term expired on January 1, 2020.

MAURICE HOWARD, FORMER MAYOR OF ABERDEEN, MISSISSIPPI

Maurice Howard was arrested in October 2019 on five counts of embezzlement of city funds. A young and charismatic mayor with a bright future is in legal trouble because of the lure of easy, but illegal, money. He has pled not guilty to the charges. In a July 2020 election, he lost his reelection bid to continue to serve as mayor of Aberdeen.

CATHERINE PUGH, FORMER MAYOR OF BALTIMORE, MARYLAND

Catherine Pugh, while in the state legislature and later as Mayor of Baltimore, implemented a creative scam to enrich herself at the expense of taxpayers, charitable organizations, businesses that dealt with the city, and even schoolchildren. Pugh self-published a series of books for children titled *Healthy Holly* and then sold tens of thousands of copies of the books to healthcare companies and charitable organizations with the promise that the books would be donated to schoolchildren. She would even sometimes require businesses that had matters pending before the city to purchase the books as a condition of doing business with the city.

Frequently, Pugh, after being paid, never delivered the books as promised; she often sold the same set of books to two different buyers and was thus paid twice. Sometimes she sold the books and never bothered to publish them, and she often kept the books and the money. The scheme garnered her over $600,000 in funds acquired by fraud and deception. The scheme was discovered when thousands of the books were found stored in a Baltimore City Public Schools warehouse; more books were found in her offices and in one of her houses. I am confident that the *Healthy Holly* books set a record for the most books that were ever sold and never read.

In May 2019, Pugh resigned as mayor of Baltimore. In a plea bargain in November 2019, Pugh pled guilty to the federal crimes of wire fraud conspiracy, conspiracy to defraud the government, and two counts of tax evasion. She was sentenced to three years in prison and three years of probation. She was ordered to pay $412,000 in restitution, forfeit $670,000, and agreed that all copies of the *Health Holly* books would be destroyed.

RICK SOLLARS, MAYOR OF TAYLOR, MICHIGAN

Rick Sollars was indicted in December 2019 in a 33-count indictment that included bribery, conspiracy to commit bribery, and wire fraud. The charges all involved public corruption in his duties as mayor. Sollars received kickbacks from a real estate developer who was awarded most of the city's tax-foreclosed properties. As of July 2020,

Sollars maintains his innocence and continues to serve as the mayor of Taylor.

TONITA GURULÉ-GIRÓN, FORMER MAYOR OF LAS VEGAS, NEW MEXICO

Tonita Gurulé-Girón did everything she could as mayor to make sure that city contracts went to her boyfriend's construction company. She has been charged with bribery and receiving kickbacks. She is accused of pressuring city employees to violate procurement procedures by ordering them to give the contracts to Gemini Construction LLC, Marvin Salazar's company (Salazar was her boyfriend). Gurulé-Girón was especially greedy—once Gemini had secured the city contracts, she unilaterally increased the amount Gemini would be paid for the work, well over the original bid, without going through the proper procedures to increase the amount. After an effort to recall the mayor, Gurulé-Girón, who pled not guilty to the charges, resigned in January 2020.

RONALD DIMURA, FORMER MAYOR OF MIDDLESEX BOROUGH, NEW JERSEY

Ronald DiMura was indicted in December 2019 on state charges of stealing more than $190,000 from political campaigns in which he served as treasurer. DiMura allegedly made donations from the campaigns to a local charitable organization he ran and then funneled the money from the charitable organization to his personal bank accounts. He is also accused of defrauding people of over $75,000 in an investment scheme. In November 2019, DiMura lost his reelection bid for mayor.

LOVELY WARREN, MAYOR OF ROCHESTER, NEW YORK

Mayor Warren is to be indicted in early October in regard to allegedly participating in and facilitating the creation of PACs to allow certain individuals to donate more than campaign limits allow. Mayor Kevin Johnson connected us via text and email. The Bureau wanted to get Mayor Lovely Warren to confirm her actions in 2017, and to see if she would direct me to this same method in exchange for a contract with her city.

EPILOGUE

As the investigation of Kevin Johnson ends, I hope I have repaid my debt to society. I have made a lot of mistakes in my life. However, every day, I continue to work and strive to do better. I am now working on building a free public safety 911 app. This is another way I am trying to give back to communities all over the country. The app will allow users to stream crimes that are taking place to local dispatchers and responding units using live video.

It was not easy for the FBI to gain access to inner corrupt political circles. I provided that access, and I hope my work will continue to lead to convictions and discourage other elected officials from using their offices for personal financial gain. Kevin will be forced to cooperate and help prosecutors close other cases.

If you work in the political space or for an elected official, and you see something or hear something off, I encourage you, especially during these crazy political times, to say something. Report it. Political corruption hurts all of us, but particularly the poor.

Most government programs are designed to help people in poverty. They rely on the government for housing, healthcare, and education. If politicians divert those funds to their own bank accounts, it makes all these programs less effective and erodes public support for the government. It increases income inequality, homelessness, and other social problems. It also discourages honest people from serving in government.

I think about all the people in the Kevin Johnson investigation who pushed back against corruption and what a difference that made. However, the politicians often made life hell for these honest government workers, and sometimes their only choices were to quit if they were not fired.

What has happened to America?

It would be a shame if the Kevin Johnsons of the world could now triumph because we are no longer shocked or outraged by their actions. If that happens, we will all be greatly diminished.

Kevin's last push in this investigation was one that did not surprise anyone. Kevin had his attorney approach me one day while I was on my daily run. When I saw him, I was immediately anxious. What the hell was about to happen?

He got out the car and told me Kevin and he were my friends, and that they knew I must have had a lot on my plate lately. They said as my friend, Kevin would like to repay me for all of my losses, including the "fine" he thought I paid. In total, this was $4.1 million. I thought about it. However, I knew it would be too much of a gamble. I could not accept money from the person I was helping to investigate. I told Kevin's attorney I needed time to think and would get back to him.

Kevin reached out to me several times via texts and calls. They all went unanswered, until one day I received a call from Kevin's attorney from a random number, saying that my mother had been at Kevin's restaurant and she had had too much to drink and needed me to come get her. Kevin's attorney said he would walk my mother over to his office, which was two buildings over, and wait for me.

After I arrived, he said she had just left to walk to her car. He said that he would show me. We got in my vehicle, and he directed me toward a park, and then to the Oak Park Community Center. He said he had just wanted to talk and apologized for taking such extreme measures. He told me he and Kevin had read my book manuscript! He bargained and begged me to take their offer, and I said I would follow up.

I did not want it. I was finally going to put this whole thing behind me, and start clean and fresh.

Yes, the mighty have fallen, but the mightier—those with true might—can build on the ruins left behind and rise again to the ideals set forth in the US Declaration of Independence, and the remarkable form of government established by the US Constitution.

Will you be part of that effort?

For me, I still must bring my own criminal case to an end. In March 2020, Special Agent Bills caught on to only one of the back doors I had built. She immediately knew why. However, she did not have a clue as to the extent of it. During this same time, another suspect in a separate investigation found out my true identity and contacted me through a third party. This person was indirectly trying to offer me a bribe to go away—the audacity. At that point, I decided it was time for me to call it a day with the FBI Sacramento office.

Some will ask why I am putting myself in jeopardy with the government. Well, one of my heroes (John Lewis) once said, "When you see something that is not right, not fair, not just, you have to speak up. You have to say something; you have to do something. Never, ever be afraid to make some noise and get in good trouble, necessary trouble."

Today, I sit at my office wrapping up my first book. These are strange times. There is no one outside of my office as I look down at the deserted streets and the park below. Coronavirus. Who would have ever figured? We just had our grand jury to indict Kevin Johnson, Toni Harp, and others, and then the world shuts down.

It is time to get back to wrapping up my own case and my own life. My passion is now picking back up on my public safety project, 911 Live. To give you a bit more info about my new app, it will be a free platform for citizens to contact fire departments, medical personnel, and police officers more easily. They will be able to call, video chat, or text message with public safety departments. Dispatchers will have the caller's precise location and can share/stream video to responding public safety members, to ensure better services and increase efficiency. It is my life's goal to continue to work on building public safety technology and giving back to my community.

As I mentioned, one thing I did notice in the end was that all the cases we pursued were those of Democrats. One would argue this could be simply because Kevin Johnson was a Democrat, and, therefore, he only introduced me to other Democrats. However, I worked many cases not related to him, and after reading this book, I would hope that you walk away at least knowing one thing for sure. That politics can be dirty.

One of the unfortunate things I have come to realize is the consequences for the front company that we used. In 2020, Government App Solutions was valued somewhere between $15 million and $20 million. Once the indictments come down, it is fair to assume the company will either be forced to close or will significantly lose its value. Who wants to invest in or do business with a company that was in the middle of a high-profile political scandal? Nor would any city want to do business with the company because of this investigation and its ties to corruption, even though the company acted innocently. Hopefully, the courts will hold Kevin and these corrupt elected officials liable for those damages and losses.

Let me conclude this book by saying the following:

As I reflect on the past few years, I have to say it has been my sincere honor and privilege to serve each and every city to help bring down corrupt elected officials. It is my hope that at the end of my final day, the people of these great cities might look back at my services and believe I left their cities just a little bit better off.

For more information about this book and to see related material, hear recordings, and more, visit www.TheMightyHaveFallen.com and www.DerekBluford.com.

PHOTO ALBUM

I have put together an album of emails, text messages, and photos that I have collected throughout my time with the Federal Bureau of Investigation. I have also found some relevant images to the investigations in which I participated in. For more, including videos and recordings, visit www.DerekBluford.com or www.TheMightyHaveFallen.com

DEREK BLUFORD

Bluford Backpack and Uniform Charity Event

Derek Bluford - FBI CHS- Texas

Derek Bluford - Winning App of the Year - TechWeek - Photo Credit to Techweek -
Photographer: Techweek

*Derek Bluford with Federal Judge after completion of court
appointment - graduation*

Derek Bluford with Mayor Kevin Johnson - State of the City - 2nd pic

Derek Bluford with Mayor Kevin Johnson at the State of the City

Derek Bluford with Shark Tank - Barbara Corcoran - Photo Credit to Shark Tank -
Photographer: uncredited

Forbes - The Top Interview with Derek Bluford - Photo Credit to Nathan
Latka (the top podcast) - Photographer: Nathan Latka

Co-working space planned in Oak Park

Jesse Jackson and Derek Bluford at Kevin Johnson event

FALL RIVER

Mayor Jasiel Correia and Elizabeth Warren - Photo Credit to Jasiel F. Correia II
(@mayorjasiel) - Photographer: Jasiel F. Correia II

Mayor Jasiel Correia Arrest - Photo Credit to The Herald News
Photographer: Ray McCullough (image taken from video)

Mayor Jasiel Correia - Photo Credit to Townsquare Media - Photographer: Barry Richard

FBI

Cash for bribes

Communication forward to FBI regarding Mayor(s) text

Derek Bluford - At FBI Scene

Derek Bluford at FBI Office

Derek Bluford at FBI Roseville Office

Derek Bluford in the field with team

FD-941 (2-26-01)

CONSENT TO SEARCH COMPUTER(S)

I, _Lodysist_ , have been asked by Special Agents of the Federal Bureau of Investigation (FBI) to permit a complete search by the FBI or its designees of any and all computers, any electronic and/or optical data storage and/or retrieval system or medium, and any related computer peripherals, described below:

iPhone 10, Apple, Model# NQCN2Ll/A, Serial number GHKWN7G9JCL6
CPU Make, Model & Serial Number (if available)

_____
Storage or Retrieval Media, Computer Peripherals

_____

and located at _____, which I own, possess, control, and/or have access to, for any evidence of a crime or other violation of the law. The required passwords, logins, and/or specific directions for computer entry are as follows: Passcode Yurman87!

I have been advised of my right to refuse to consent to this search, and I give permission for this search, freely and voluntarily, and not as the result of threats or promises of any kind.

I authorize those Agents to take any evidence discovered during this search, together with the medium in/on which it is stored, and any associated data, hardware, software and computer peripherals.

11/13/19
Date

11/13/19
Date

Signature

Signature of Witness

Rachael LaChapelle
Printed Full Name of Witness

_____
Location

FBI - Consent Form to dump phone - Special Agent Rachael La'Chapelle

11:20

✕ Consent forms.pdf

FD-941 (2-26-01)

CONSENT TO SEARCH COMPUTER(S)

I, ___*Rebbapart*___ , have been asked by Special Agents of the

Federal Bureau of Investigation (FBI) to permit a complete search by the FBI or its designees of any and all computers,

any electronic and/or optical data storage and/or retrieval system or medium, and any related computer peripherals,

described below:

___iPhone 11___
CPU Make, Model & Serial Number (if available)

___IMEI 35 324 310 141 553 5___
Storage or Retrieval Media, Computer Peripherals

and located at _____ , which I own, possess,

control, and/or have access to, for any evidence of a crime or other violation of the law. The required passwords, logins,

and/or specific directions for computer entry are as follows: ___Yurman87'___ .

    I have been advised of my right to refuse to consent to this search, and I give permission for this search, freely

and voluntarily, and not as the result of threats or promises of any kind.

    I authorize those Agents to take any evidence discovered during this search, together with the medium in/on which

it is stored, and any associated data, hardware, software and computer peripherals.

___12/12/19___
Date

___12/12/19___
Date

___*Rebbapart*___
Signature

___Rebekah D Bills___
Signature of Witness

___Rebekah L. Bills___
Printed Full Name of Witness

___912 Pleasant Grove Blvd___
Location ___Roseville, CA 95678___

FBI - Consent Form to dump phone - Special Agent Rebekah Bills

168

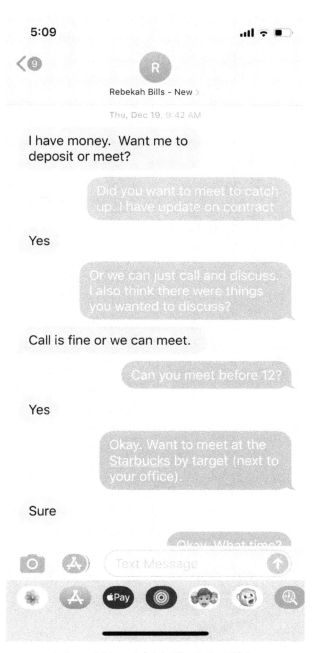

FBI - Special Agent Rebekah Bills - Paying Lobbyist

FBI - Special Agent Rebekah Bills - Pitch to keep things going financially

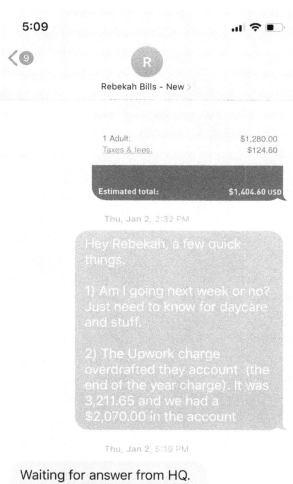

5:09

Rebekah Bills - New ⟩

| 1 Adult: | $1,280.00 |
| Taxes & fees: | $124.60 |

Estimated total: $1,404.60 USD

Thu, Jan 2, 2:32 PM

Hey Rebekah, a few quick things.

1) Am I going next week or no? Just need to know for daycare and stuff.

2) The Upwork charge overdrafted they account (the end of the year charge). It was 3,211.65 and we had a $2,070.00 in the account

Thu, Jan 2, 5:19 PM

Waiting for answer from HQ. Trying to get funds out tomorrow

Fri, Jan 3, 9:02 AM

Text Message

FBI - Special Agent Rebekah Bills - Reimbursement

171

5:13

Rebekah Bills - New

Ok, I think later today just email KJ that you will stop by the restaurant tonight if he will be there. Tell him you heard back from Harp but have some questions about moving forward. Also try to call Svante.

Tonight will be hard. We just got called into a management meeting - my boss was let go

It would just need to be late

Ok can try tomorrow

Ok

I can still
Meet you tonight to give you phone though

Ok

Mon, Oct 28, 2:41 PM

He's trying to call me. FYI.

Text Message

FBI - Special Agent Rebekah Bills - Requesting The Lobbyist to follow Mayor Kevin Johnson

5:21

RB

Rebekah ›

Mon, Jul 22, 2:04 PM

Hi Rebekah. Kevin's attorney sent me an updated agreement for the additional shares for making more introductions. What's your email address so I can forward it to you?

rlbills@fbi.gov

Call me when you can please

Tue, Jul 30, 11:14 AM

Update on dates?

Not yet. I'll call him today after work.

Ok. Are there better dates for you? We can push it out anytime in Aug. Let me know.

No. I already put in for those days off

Next week? Which days

Text Message

FBI - Special Agent Rebekah Bills confirming email address

FBI - Special Agent Rebekah Bills confirming Lindsay Farrells number with The Lobbyist

FBI - Special Agent Rebekah Bills purchasing gift cards with other campaigns

FBI - Special Agent Rebekah Bills shares Mayor Kevin Johnson SNR article with the Lobbyist

FBI Camcorder Watch 1 of 2

FBI Camcorder Watch 2 of 2

FBI CHS Derek Bluford

FBI controlled online contribution - gift card - 1 of 2

FBI controlled online contribution - gift card - 2 of 2

FBI Recording Device - Nano Eagle

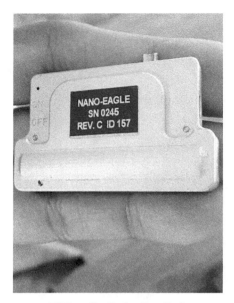

FBI Recording Device - Nano Eagle

FBI recording Device issued in New York

5:07

Rebekah Bills - New >

Fri, Jan 17, 2:36 PM

What is the code to get into the parking lot at KJ's office?

It was on my old phone and for some reason all of my kJ stuff didn't transfer over

Okay

He did say that he'll give us the codes and stuff at this meeting

Sounds good. Thanks

Sat, Jan 18, 12:52 PM

Did you send message?

FBI Special Agent Rebekah Bills requesting Mayor Johnsons gate code

FBI Tie - Hidden Camera

FBI Tie Camera

184

New York FBI Office

Special Agent Rebekah Bills - Reimbursement Accounting

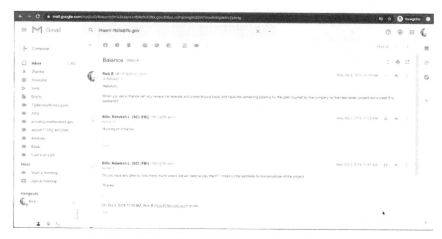

Special Agent Bills emailing CHS Bluford regarding development work

Special Agent Rebekah Bills _ CHS Derek Bluford discussing Kevin Johnson communication. Kevin informing Derek Bluford that he can get the Mayors to deliever the contracts

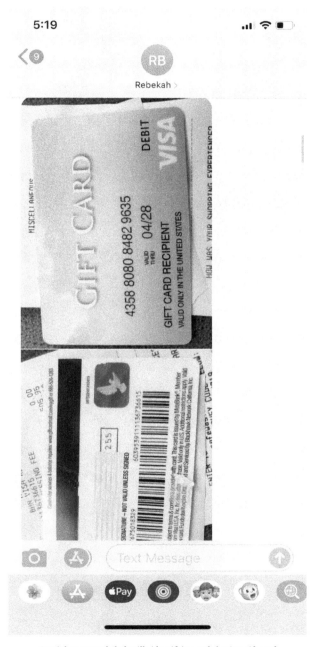

Special Agent Rebekah Bills identifying and sharing gift card information with CHS Bluford to use for online contributions - 2 of 2

*Special Agent Rebekah Bills informing CHS Bluford to download a
secondary phone recorder*

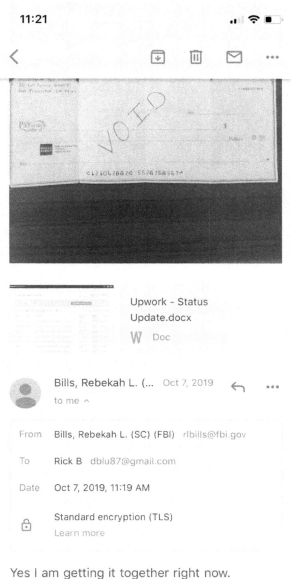

The Lobbyist requesting reimbursement from the FBI 2 of 2

FONTANA - MAYOR ACQUANETTA WARREN

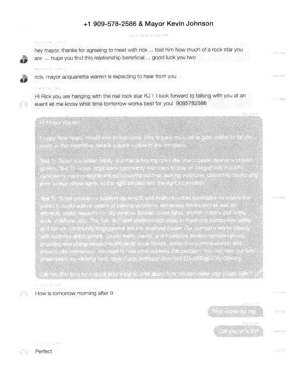

Mayor Kevin Johnson & Mayor Acquanetta Warren & CHS Derek Bluford

10:55 ✈

Re: Introduction: Mayor Warren from Fontana <> Rick Gov App Solutions

☆

me Jun 4, 2018
to Robert, bcc: 4488783 ⌃

↩ ...

From	Rick Lavon rick@govappsolutions.com
To	Robert Ramsey rramsey@fontana.org
Bcc	4488783@bcc.hubspot.com
Date	Jun 4, 2018, 11:2...

Hi Chief Ramsey,

I hope this email finds you doing well. I just wanted to circle back with you. Mayor Acquanetta made an introduction to us earlier this year regarding both our Texting & Driving and Parking Enforcement program. I know that you are very busy, but I wanted to see if now was a better time to meet with you or someone from your team regarding our programs?

I've attached some additional information below. I hope that you have a great week and I look forward to your response!

Parking Enforcement Demo: https://vimeo.com/270484760
Texting & Driving Demo: https://vimeo.com/270491328

Best regards,

Rick Lavon
Rick@GovAppSolutions.com

Fontana

5:25

MW K

2 People >

Text Message
Tue, Dec 3, 2:59 PM

Kj - new

mayor, just following up to connect you with rick from gov app. rick, as you know, mayor warren is a rock star! will let you both take it from here.

Tue, Dec 3, 5:22 PM

Mayor Warren,

Pleasure to meet you. Would love to find a time to tell you about our public safety technology and how we are helping cities become safer while helping their homeless community. Do you have any available time this month to meet?

Mayor Acquanetta Warren

Hi let me check

Mon, Jan 6, 12:41 PM

Text Message

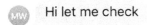

Mayor Johnson introducing FBI CHS Derek Bluford to Mayor Warren

KEVIN JOHNSON

Office of the Mayor - Photo Credit to The Sacramento Bee
Photographer: Staff Photo (Bryan Patrick was the photographer)

Hillary Clinton and Mayor Kevin Johnson at USCM - Photo Credit to
Kevin Johnson (@KJ_MayorJohnson) - Photographer: Kevin Johnson

Hillary Clinton and Mayor Kevin Johnson - Photo Credit to Getty Images - Photographer: Justin Sullivan

Jesse Jackson and Mayor Kevin Johnson

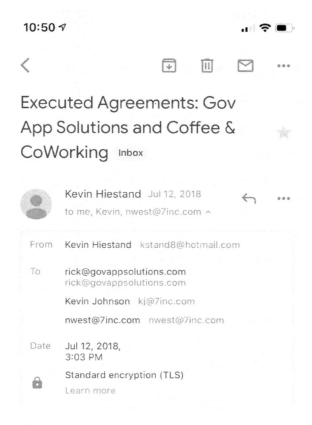

10:50 ⏎

Executed Agreements: Gov App Solutions and Coffee & CoWorking Inbox

Kevin Hiestand Jul 12, 2018
to me, Kevin, nwest@7inc.com ⌄

From	Kevin Hiestand kstand8@hotmail.com
To	rick@govappsolutions.com
	rick@govappsolutions.com
	Kevin Johnson kj@7inc.com
	nwest@7inc.com nwest@7inc.com
Date	Jul 12, 2018, 3:03 PM
🔒	Standard encryption (TLS)
	Learn more

Rick:

Attached for your records are final executed copies of the following:

1.) Consulting Agreement between Seven Ventures, Inc and Gov App Solutions

2.) Partnership Agreement between Seven Ventures, Inc. and Gov App Solutions.

Let me know if you have any questions.

•••
━━━━━━━━━━━

Kevin Johnson and his attorney Kevin Hiestand sending over updated contracts 1 of 2

10:50 ⌐

Kevin Johnson   kj@7inc.com

nwest@7inc.com   nwest@7inc.com

Date   Jul 12, 2018,
3:03 PM

🔒   Standard encryption (TLS)
Learn more

Rick:

Attached for your records are final executed copies of the following:

1.) Consulting Agreement between Seven Ventures, Inc and Gov App Solutions

2.) Partnership Agreement between Seven Ventures, Inc. and Gov App Solutions.

Let me know if you have any questions.

•••

Kevin

Exec.Consult.Agr.
7.12.18.pdf
📄 PDF

Executed.Partner
ship.Agr.7.12.18....
📄 PDF

↩ Reply   ⟨⟨ Reply all   ↪ Forward

Kevin Johnson and his attorney Kevin Hiestand sending over updated contracts 2 of 2

CONSULTING AGREEMENT

Government App Solutions, Inc., is a California Corporation ("Client"), and Seven Ventures, Inc., a California corporation dba Seven, Inc. ("Consultant"), effective as of, July 1, 2018 ("Effective Date"), agree as follows:

1.   Background and Purpose. Client and its associated entities have established a crowdsourcing platform for municipalities to increase road safety, community living, ordinance management and decrease distracted driver incidents. Consultant has extensive background and experience in performing services related to the scope of services set forth in this Consulting Agreement ("Agreement").

2.   Consulting Services. Client contracts for the services of Consultant, and Consultant agrees to provide consulting services to Client, on the terms and conditions set forth below.

3.   Independent Contractor. The parties agree that Consultant shall perform all services required hereunder as an independent contractor, and not as an employee, agent, joint venturer or partner of Client for any purpose whatsoever. Except as expressly provided herein, Client shall have no right to, and shall not, control the manner or prescribe the method by which Consultant performs the consulting services hereunder. Consultant shall be entirely and solely responsible for Consultant's acts while engaged in the performance of such consulting services. Consultant shall provide Consultant's own equipment, including computers and software, necessary for Consultant to provide the services under this Agreement. The employees and agents of each party shall not be considered employees or agents of the other for any purpose.

4.   Scope of Services. During the term of this Agreement, Consultant shall provide the services specified on the Scope of Work attached hereto as **Exhibit A**.

4.1.   Time and Effort. Client acknowledges that Consultant may provide services to a number of other businesses. Client agrees that Consultant is free to engage in such other business so long as such engagement does not unreasonably interfere with the duties set forth in this Agreement. Consultant shall devote as much time to the performance of the consulting services under this Agreement as is reasonably necessary for the performance of such services.

4.2.   Best Efforts; Applicable Laws. Consultant shall devote Consultant's best efforts, attention, skill and experience in providing the consulting services. All services performed by Consultant shall be in accordance with all applicable federal, state and local laws and all applicable regulations regarding such services.

4.3.   Records, Reporting and Audits. Consultant shall maintain accurate records of all matters that relate to Consultant's obligations under this Agreement. Consultant shall retain such records for a period of three years from the date of final payment under this Agreement and shall provide copies to Client as may be requested by Client from time-to-time.

1

Kevin Johnson contract for LA, Phoenix and New Haven - Executed Page 1 of 7

PHOTO ALBUM

5.   Compensation & Revenue Sharing. For services rendered hereunder, Client shall pay Consultant as follows:

       i.   an annual retainer of one-dollar ($1) payable during the term of this Agreement;

       ii.   revenue sharing as set forth in **Exhibit B** attached hereto. Client represents and warrants that Client has all power, rights and authority to approve and grant the revenue sharing set forth on **Exhibit B**.

5.1   Expenses. In addition, Client shall reimburse Consultant for Consultant's reasonable out-of-pocket expenses incurred in connection with this Agreement, provided that Client has approved in writing any single such expense greater than $1,000 or each and every expense that would require Client to reimburse Consultant more than $2,000, in the aggregate, during the term of this Agreement, prior to Consultant incurring such expense.

5.2   Reporting, Books and Records for Payment. Within sixty (60) days of the end of Client's reporting period (based on a calendar year) following the first sale of Client's product to, or strategic investment with, a municipality occurring as a result of Consultant's efforts and within sixty (60) days after the end of each annual period thereafter, Client shall make a written report to Consultant setting forth that information necessary to permit Consultant to calculate and confirm the revenue share payment due Consultant, even if no payment is due.

Client shall keep, and shall cause its Affiliates to keep, books and records in such reasonable detail as will permit the reports provided for in this Section to be made and the revenue share payable hereunder to be determined. Client further agrees to permit its and its Affiliates' books and records to be inspected and audited from time to time (but not more often than once annually) during reasonable business hours by an independent auditor, designated by Consultant and approved by Client, which approval will not be unreasonably withheld, to the extent necessary to verify the reports provided for in this Section; provided, however, that such auditor shall indicate to Consultant only whether the reports and revenue share paid are correct, and if not, the reason why not. In the event that such an audit results in additional revenue share being owed to Consultant, such amount shall be paid within twenty (20) days from a written notice of deficiency.

6.   Term and Termination of Agreement. This Agreement shall commence on the Effective Date and shall continue through _____, unless mutually agreed upon in writing by both parties to extend the Agreement.

7.   Confidential Data.
7.1.   Each party will hold in complete confidence and not disclose produce, publish, permit access to, or reveal any Confidential Information of the other party, at any time prior to the other party's intentional public disclosure of such information, without the express prior

2

Kevin Johnson contract for LA, Phoenix and New Haven - Executed Page 2 of 7

written consent of the other party. Upon the written request of a party, the other party will return or destroy materials prepared by such party that contain Confidential Information. Disclosure of Confidential Information is not precluded if such disclosure is in response to a valid order of a court or other governmental body of the United States or any political subdivision thereof; provided that the party ordered to provide the Confidential Information give notice to the other party and make a reasonable effort to obtain a protective order requiring that the Confidential Information be disclosed only for limited purposes for which the order was issued. A party shall use the Confidential Information only for the limited purpose for which it was disclosed.

    7.2.   Definition of Confidential Information. "Confidential Information" means all information and material which is confidential or proprietary to a party, whether or not marked as "confidential" or "proprietary" and which is disclosed to or obtained by the other party, which is related to such party's past, present or further activities and which such party advises the other party is confidential or by its nature would be assumed to be confidential. Confidential Information does not include any information which (a) was in the lawful and unrestricted possession of a party prior to its disclosure by the other party; (b) is or becomes generally available to the public by acts other than those of the other party after receiving it; or (c) has been received lawfully and in good faith by the other party from a third party who did not derive it from the party owning the Confidential Information or subject to a non-disclosure obligation.

    8.   Cooperation. The parties shall cooperate fully with each other to enable each party to perform its duties under this Agreement. Each party shall provide the other with all relevant information and documents. Client shall make appropriate Client representatives available for meetings, consultations and conversations.

    9.   Indemnification. Each party ("Indemnitor") agrees to indemnify, defend and hold the other ("Indemnitee") harmless from any loss, cost, liability, claim, expense, penalty or fine, including attorneys' fees (without regard to whether litigation is commenced) suffered or incurred, directly or indirectly, as a result of any material breach by Indemnitor of any of Indemnitor's representations, warranties, covenants or obligations contained in this Agreement. Indemnitee shall promptly notify Indemnitor of the existence of any matter to which the indemnification obligations would apply and shall give Indemnitor a reasonable opportunity to defend at Indemnitor's own expense and with counsel of Indemnitor's own selection; provided that Indemnitee shall at all times also have the right to fully participate in the defense at Indemnitee's own expense.

    10.   Resolution of Disputes.

    10.1.   Definition of Disputes. Any claim or controversy arising out of or pertaining to this Agreement ("Dispute") shall be resolved as provided in this Section. The parties agree that no party shall have the right to sue any other party regarding a Dispute except as provided in this Section.

    10.2.   Negotiation. If a Dispute arises between the parties, they shall use their best efforts for a period of at least thirty (30) days to resolve the Dispute by negotiation. To commence the Dispute resolution process, any party shall serve written notice on the other

3

Kevin Johnson contract for LA, Phoenix and New Haven - Executed Page 3 of 7

party, as provided by Section 11.3, specifically identifying the Dispute and requesting that efforts at resolving the Dispute begin.

10.3. Binding Arbitration. If the parties' good faith efforts at resolving the Dispute by agreement through negotiation are unsuccessful within the thirty (30) day period following commencement of negotiation, the Dispute shall be submitted to, and conclusively determined by, binding arbitration before either JAMS or AAA in Sacramento, California. The provisions of this Section shall not preclude any party from seeking injunctive or other provisional or equitable relief in order to preserve the status quo of the parties pending resolution of the Dispute. The filing of an action seeking injunctive or other provisional relief or specific performance shall not be construed as a waiver of that party's arbitration rights.

11.   Miscellaneous.

11.1. Amendment. The provisions of this Agreement may be modified at any time by agreement of the parties. Any such agreement hereafter made shall be ineffective to modify this Agreement in any respect unless in writing and signed by the parties against whom enforcement of the modification or discharge is sought.

11.2. Waiver. Any of the terms or conditions of this Agreement may be waived at any time by the party entitled to the benefit thereof, but no such waiver shall affect or impair the right of the waiving party to require observance, performance or satisfaction either of that term or condition as it applies on a subsequent occasion or of any other term or condition.

11.3. Notices. Any notice under this Agreement shall be in writing, and any written notice or other document shall be deemed to have been duly given (i) on the date of personal service on the parties, (ii) on the third business day after mailing, if the document is mailed by registered or certified mail, (iii) one day after being sent by professional or overnight courier or messenger service guaranteeing oneday delivery, with receipt confirmed by the courier, or (iv) on the date of transmission if sent by telegram, telex, telecopy or other means of electronic transmission resulting in written copies, with receipt confirmed. Any such notice shall be delivered or addressed to the parties at the addresses set forth below or at the most recent address specified by the addressee through written notice under this provision. Failure to conform to the requirement that mailings be done by registered or certified mail shall not defeat the effectiveness of notice actually received by the addressee.

11.4. Attorneys' Fees; Prejudgment Interest. If the services of an attorney are required by any party to secure the performance of this Agreement or otherwise upon the breach or default of another party to this Agreement, or if any judicial remedy or arbitration is necessary to enforce or interpret any provision of this Agreement or the rights and duties of any person in relation thereto, the prevailing party shall be entitled to reasonable attorneys' fees, costs and other expenses, in addition to any other relief to which such party may be entitled. Any award of damages following judicial remedy or arbitration as a result of the breach of this Agreement or any of its provisions shall include an award of prejudgment interest from the date of the breach at the maximum amount of interest allowed by law.

11.5. Severability. If any provision of this Agreement is held by a court of competent jurisdiction to be invalid or unenforceable, the remainder of the Agreement which

4

Kevin Johnson contract for LA, Phoenix and New Haven - Executed Page 4 of 7

can be given effect without the invalid provision shall continue in full force and effect and shall in no way be impaired or invalidated.

11.6. Entire Agreement. This document and its exhibits constitute the entire agreement between the parties, all oral agreements being merged herein, and supersede all prior representations. There are no representations, agreements, arrangements, or understandings, oral or written, between or among the parties relating to the subject matter of this Agreement that are not fully expressed herein or therein.

11.7. Governing Law. The rights and obligations of the parties and the interpretation and performance of this Agreement shall be governed by the law of California, excluding its conflict of laws rules.

11.8. Assignability. Neither party shall assign this Agreement, or interest therein, without the prior written consent of the other party, such consent shall not unreasonably be withheld. No such assignment shall release the assigning party from its obligations and liabilities hereunder unless specifically agreed to in writing.

11.9. Liability. It is intended by the parties to this Agreement that Client's and Consultant's obligations in connection with the Services shall not subject Client's or Consultant's employees, officers, members, partners, lenders or representatives to any personal legal exposure from the risks associated with this Agreement. Therefore, and notwithstanding anything to the contrary contained herein, Consultant and Client agree that as Consultant's and Client's sole and exclusive remedy, any claims demand or suit shall be directed and/or asserted only against Client or Consultant, as the case may be, and not against any of Client's or Consultant's employees, officers, members, partners, lenders or representatives.

Client:

Government App Solutions, Inc.

By: _Dssa Behrl_

Address: _3428 5' Ave_
Sacramento, CA 95817

Consultant:

Seven Ventures, Inc.

By: _____
     Kevin Johnson, President

Address: P.O. Box 5757
         Sacramento, CA 95817

5

Kevin Johnson contract for LA, Phoenix and New Haven - Executed Page 5 of 7

Exhibit A

Scope of Work

Consultant shall familiarize itself with all facets of the Client's Product and introduce Client to municipalities interested in Client's product. Consultant's tasks, goals and deliverables shall include, but not necessarily be limited to the following:

(a) assist Client in securing a financial or strategic investment from the following municipalities: Los Angeles, California; Phoenix, Arizona; and New Haven, Connecticut; among others;

(b) advise and recommend other assistance leading to the securing of financial or strategic investments from municipalities;

(e) such consulting services as the Client may reasonably request in connection with the development of its product.

6

Kevin Johnson contract for LA, Phoenix and New Haven - Executed Page 6 of 7

Exhibit B

<u>Revenue Sharing</u>

Upon satisfaction of the performance goals specified below, Client (or the appropriate affiliate of Client) shall award Consultant revenue sharing payments under the following terms as follows:

i.   Consultant shall be entitled to and is due to receive revenue sharing in such amounts of a total of seventeen percent (17%) of all current and future net revenues specifically generated from Client's partnership, either financially or strategically based, with the City of Los Angeles; and

ii.   Consultant shall be entitled to and is due to receive revenue sharing in such amounts of a total of ten percent (10%) of all current and future net revenues specifically generated from Client's partnership, either financially or strategically based, with the City of Phoenix, Arizona; and

iii.   Consultant shall be entitled to and is due to receive revenue sharing in such amounts of a total of ten percent (10%) of all current and future net revenues specifically generated from Client's partnership, either financially or strategically based, with the City of New Haven, Connecticut.

7

Kevin Johnson contract for LA, Phoenix and New Haven - Executed Page 7 of 7

Kevin Johnson Phone Log

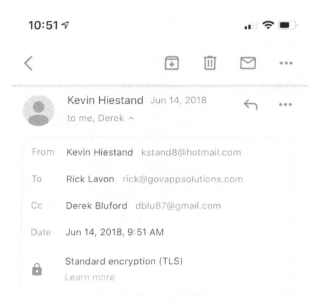

10:51

From Kevin Hiestand kstand8@hotmail.com

To Rick Lavon rick@govappsolutions.com

Cc Derek Bluford dblu87@gmail.com

Date Jun 14, 2018, 9:51 AM

Standard encryption (TLS)
Learn more

Rick:

Hope you're feeling better.

Just following up on our brief meeting on Monday concerning Kevin J.'s work with your various entities. You should have all docs pertaining to Gov App Solutions. Let me know the status of those.

Attached is a consulting agreement whereby Coffee and Coworking grants a 5% equity membership to Kevin for advise, etc. I don't know what type of legal entity Coffee and Coworking is, so we might need to make a ʼange. Let me know your thoughts.

ꟲ

ʼons attorney confirming interest in numerous entities

Mayor Kevin Johnson _ Derek Bluford discussing SeedInvest

Mayor Kevin Johnson & Michelle Rhee-Johnson - Photo Credit to Grand
Gala (webpage active from 2001 to 2019, event was Kentucky Derby) -
Photographer: Grand Gala

Mayor Kevin Johnson & NBA Commissioner Donald Stern - Photo
Credit to The Sacramento Bee - Photographer: Jose Luis Villegas

Mayor Kevin Johnson and Derek Bluford - Sacramento

Mayor Kevin Johnson and Derek Bluford

Mayor Kevin Johnson, CHS Derek Bluford and other in New York

Mayor Kevin Johnson, CHS Derek Bluford and other

Mayor Kevin Johnson, Derek Bluford and other at Fixins Restaurant
grand opening in Sacramento

Nancy Pelosi, Mayor Kevin Johnson, and Michelle Rhee - Photo Credit to Daily Bail - Photographer: Staff Photo

National Conference of Black Mayors - Photo Credit to City of Sacramento – Office of Mayor Kevin Johnson - Photographer: City of Sacramento – Office of Mayor Kevin Johnson

President Barack Obama and Kevin Johnson at White House - Photo Credit to Reuters - Photographer: Kevin Lamarque

President Barack Obama and Mayor Kevin Johnson - Photo Credit to NBC Photographer: Staff Photographer (on photo, bottom right corner)

President Donald Trump and Mayor Kevin Johnson and Michelle Rhee
-Photo Credit to The Associated Press Photographer: Carolyn Kaster

LOS ANGELES

Chief Hale abrupt exit email from LADOT 1 of 2

11:04 ⏎

have come to know and work with so many amazing
people. The unexpected opportunity to serve as the
Interim Chief has been especially gratifying. However,
there comes a time for all us when you feel "it is
time." So after a public service career of 45 years, I have
decided that now is that time.

It has been my pleasure to work with all of you. Thank
you for being such a dedicated and supportive partner.
Together, we were able to achieve some memorable
accomplishments.

In sincere gratitude,
Brian

--

Brian Hale

Chief / Executive Officer
Parking Enforcement and Traffic Control
Division

Los Angeles Department of Transportation

213.972. 8426.

*****************Confidentiality Notice*********************

Notice: The information contained in this message is
proprietary information belonging to the City of Los
Angeles and/or its Proprietary Departments and is
intended only for the confidential use of the addressee.

Chief Hale abrupt exit email from LADOT 2 of 2

11:08 ⏱

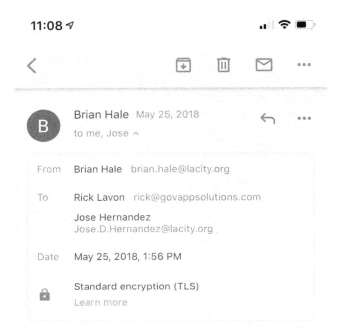

Brian Hale May 25, 2018
to me, Jose ⌃

From	Brian Hale brian.hale@lacity.org
To	Rick Lavon rick@govappsolutions.com
	Jose Hernandez Jose.D.Hernandez@lacity.org
Date	May 25, 2018, 1:56 PM
🔒	Standard encryption (TLS) Learn more

Hi Rick,
Sorry for my tardiness in responding to your email sent earlier
this week. I did receive information the Mayor's Office would
like us to explore opportunities for deploying your application.
I have also spoken with a manager in my Parking Support
Group about your product. I have looped in Jose Hernandez,
who can help coordinate a meeting for our further discussion.

Have a great weekend,
Brian

● ● ●

me May 25, 2018
Hi Brian, Thanks for the email. No worries at all....

me Jun 1, 2018
Hi All, I hope that you both had a great week. Ju...

me Jun 13, 2018
Hi Brian & Jose, Hope all is going well. I wanted...

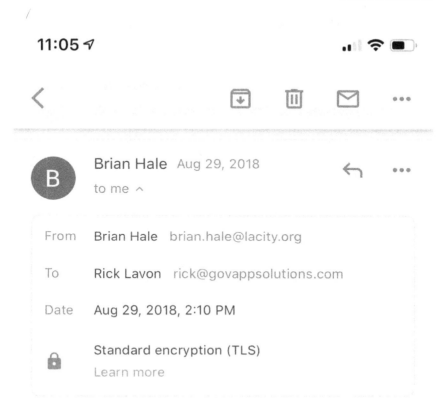

11:05

From   Brian Hale   brian.hale@lacity.org

To   Rick Lavon   rick@govappsolutions.com

Date   Aug 29, 2018, 2:10 PM

Standard encryption (TLS)
Learn more

Thanks for the kind words. Devon Farfan will be taking the lead on this project (cc'd). She is familiar with the GAS proposal and some of the details we discussed.   We also had our bi-weekly meeting with Conduent today and some data was presented for our consideration.

Best wishes,
Brian

Chief Hale from LADOT passing us over to Chief Farfan

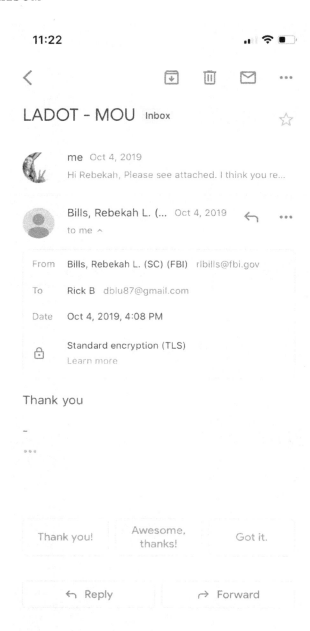

FBI requesting a copy of the LADOT MOU

Gift cards purchased to use as campaign contribution money

Kevin Johnson confirming plan with Mayor Garcetti via email. Forwarded to FBI

Mayor Kevin Johnson, NoelVasquez - Photo Credit to Getty Images - Photographer: Noel Vasquez

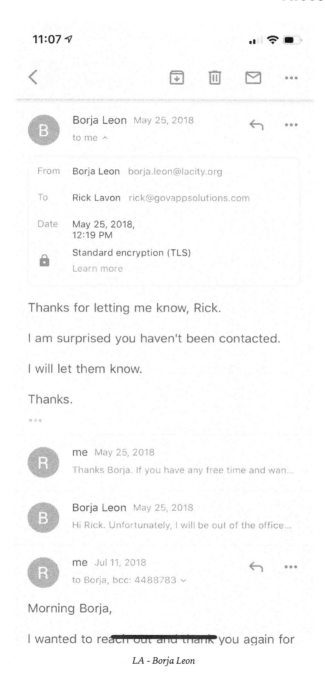

LA - Borja Leon

LA Director of Transportation - Borja Leon

LADOT Chief Brian Hale signing the agreement to do services

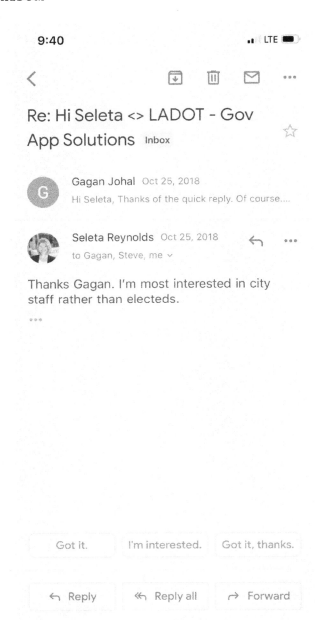

LADOT Seleta Reynolds emailing the company

Mayor Eric Garcetti and Mayor Kevin Johnson - Photo Credit to Kevin Johnson (@KJ_MayorJohnson) - Photographer: Kevin Johnson

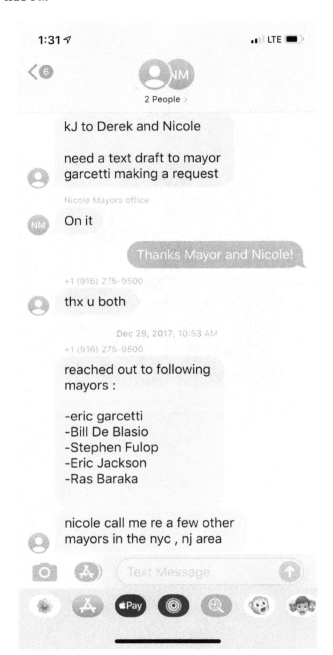

Mayor Johnson confirming that he reached out to Mayor Eric Garcetti, Mayor Bill De Blasio, Mayor Stephen Fulop, Mayor Eric Jackson, and Mayor Ras Baraka

Mayor Kevin Johnson & Nicole

FROM DEREK

I'm going to be in Los Angeles next week. Do you think you could get me in with anyone from the mayors office for parking enforcement?

kJ to Derek and Nicole

need a text draft to mayor garcetti making a request

On it

Thanks Mayor and Nicole!

thx u both

reached out to following mayors :

-eric garcetti
-Bill De Blasio
-Stephen Fulop
-Eric Jackson
-Ras Baraka

nicole call me re a few other mayors in the nyc , nj area

Thanks. And just for your records, your should know that we have had two successful meetings with both Stockton and City of Sacramento rescheduled for this 12th)

nicole what was status of Cabaldon, west sac

Elk Grove
Roseville
Folsom

u want any of these above ?

Yes

All of the above would work

Mayor Kevin Johnson - FBI CHS Derek Bluford

227

Mayor Kevin Johnson and Mayor Eric Garcetti in LA - Photo Credit to Getty Images -
Photographer: Noel Vasquez

Mayor Kevin Johnson and Mayor Eric Garcetti - Photo Credit to Getty Images -
Photographer: Andrew D. Bernstein

Mayor Kevin Johnson giving update on Mayor Eric Garcetti

MISCELLANEOUS

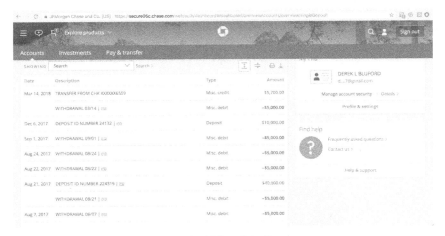

Cash Withdrawals 1 of 2

Cash Withdrawals 2 of 2

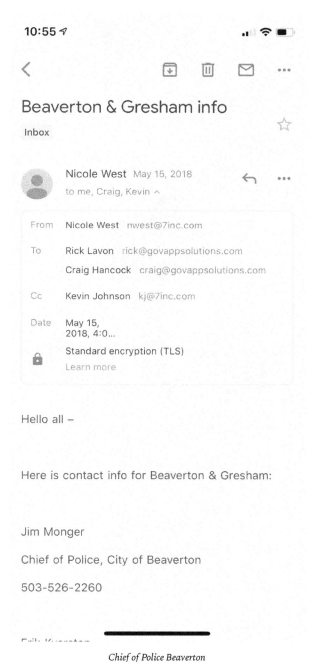

10:55

Beaverton & Gresham info

Inbox

Nicole West May 15, 2018
to me, Craig, Kevin

From	Nicole West nwest@7inc.com
To	Rick Lavon rick@govappsolutions.com
	Craig Hancock craig@govappsolutions.com
Cc	Kevin Johnson kj@7inc.com
Date	May 15, 2018, 4:0...
🔒	Standard encryption (TLS) Learn more

Hello all –

Here is contact info for Beaverton & Gresham:

Jim Monger

Chief of Police, City of Beaverton

503-526-2260

Erik Kvarsten

Chief of Police Beaverton

Derek Bluford - US Marshals Office

Derek Bluford - US Marshals Offices

Derek Bluford and Tracy Stigler

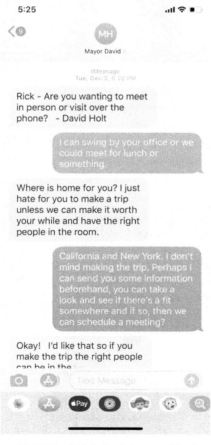

FBI CHS Derek Bluford and Mayor David Holt

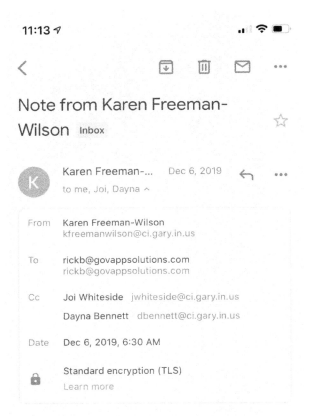

11:13

Note from Karen Freeman-Wilson Inbox

K Karen Freeman-... Dec 6, 2019
to me, Joi, Dayna

From Karen Freeman-Wilson
kfreemanwilson@ci.gary.in.us

To rickb@govappsolutions.com
rickb@govappsolutions.com

Cc Joi Whiteside jwhiteside@ci.gary.in.us
Dayna Bennett dbennett@ci.gary.in.us

Date Dec 6, 2019, 6:30 AM

Standard encryption (TLS)
Learn more

Good morning Rick. Hope you are well. I am following up on the text from Mayor Kevin Johnson. I am adding my assistant Joi Whiteside to set a meeting in the next two weeks. I would also ask that she add Jeff Willams from the incoming administration. Thank you for your interest. Karen

Sent from my iPhone

_____
_____ This email and any files transmitted with it are the sole property of the City of Gary and/or its affiliates, are confidential and are intended solely for the

Gary Indiana Mayor Karen Freeman-Wilson

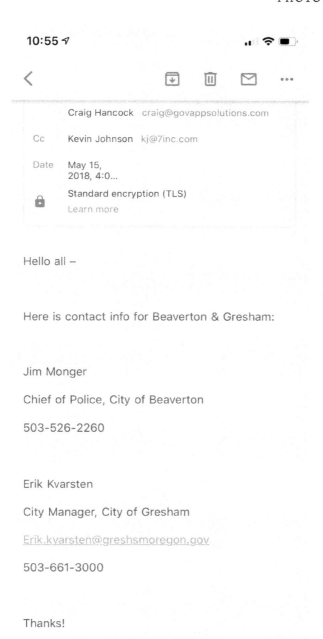

10:55

Craig Hancock   craig@govappsolutions.com

Cc   Kevin Johnson   kj@7inc.com

Date   May 15,
        2018, 4:0...

🔒   Standard encryption (TLS)
        Learn more

Hello all –

Here is contact info for Beaverton & Gresham:

Jim Monger

Chief of Police, City of Beaverton

503-526-2260

Erik Kvarsten

City Manager, City of Gresham

Erik.kvarsten@greshsmoregon.gov

503-661-3000

Thanks!

——————

Gresham Oregon - City Manager

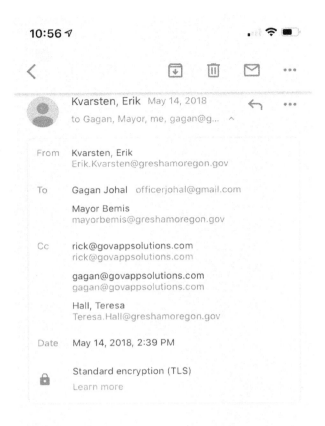

10:56

From   Kvarsten, Erik
        Erik.Kvarsten@greshamoregon.gov

To   Gagan Johal   officerjohal@gmail.com

        Mayor Bemis
        mayorbemis@greshamoregon.gov

Cc   rick@govappsolutions.com
        rick@govappsolutions.com

        gagan@govappsolutions.com
        gagan@govappsolutions.com

        Hall, Teresa
        Teresa.Hall@greshamoregon.gov

Date   May 14, 2018, 2:39 PM

        Standard encryption (TLS)
        Learn more

Gagan,

I'll have Teresa Hall from my office, find a convenient time to visit.

Regards,

Erik Kvarsten, City Manager | City of Gresham

Gresham City Manager Responding

11:59

LTE

2 People

Text Message
Yesterday 2:57 PM

+1 (916) 900-1022

mayor, just following up to connect you with rick from gov app. rick, as you know, mayor bemis is a rock star! will let you both take it from here.

Yesterday 5:22 PM

Mayor Bemis,

Pleasure to meet you. Would love to find a time to tell you about our public safety technology and how we are helping cities become safer while helping their homeless community. Do you have any available time this month to meet?

Text Message

Pay

Kevin Johnson introducing CHS Derek Bluford to Mayor Bemis

11:59 ⏁   ..ıLTE ☐

‹8   2 People ›

Text Message
Monday 6:24 PM

+1 (916) 900-1022

mayor, just following up to connect you with rick from gov app. rick, mayor freeman-wilson is a rock star! will let you both take it from here.
rick's e-mail:
rickb@govappsolutions.com

+1 (219) 293-5329

Thank you Mayor! Rick look forward to connecting. Please stand by for my email.

Mayor Freeman Wilson,

Pleasure to meet you. Would love to find a time to tell you about our public safety technology and how we are helping cities become safer while helping their homeless community. Do you have any available time this month to meet?

Kevin Johnson introducing CHS Derek Bluford to Mayor Freeman-Wilson

238

11:58 ⏱   ⬤⬤⬤ LTE ▭

‹ 8   2 People ›

+1 (916) 900-1022

mayor, just following up to
connect you with rick from gov
app. rick, as you know, mayor
holt is a rock star! will let you
both take it from here.

Yesterday 5:22 PM

Mayor Holt,

Pleasure to meet you. Would
love to find a time to tell you
about our public safety
technology and how we are
helping cities become safer
while helping their homeless
community. Do you have any
available time this month to
meet?

Yesterday 8:19 PM

Maybe: David Holt

Thanks, KJ!
Rick - I'll take us over to a
separate text to spare Mayor
Johnson.

Kevin Johnson introducing CHS Derek Bluford to Mayor Holt

< 8

2 People >

Text Message
Yesterday 2:59 PM

+1 (916) 900-1022

mayor, just following up to connect you with rick from gov app. rick, as you know, mayor warren is a rock star! will let you both take it from here.

Yesterday 5:22 PM

Mayor Warren,

Pleasure to meet you. Would love to find a time to tell you about our public safety technology and how we are helping cities become safer while helping their homeless community. Do you have any available time this month to meet?

+1 (909) 578-2586

Hi let me check

Kevin Johnson introducing CHS Derek Bluford to Mayor Warren

11:59 ✐   ▪▫ LTE 🔋

‹ 8   👥
                          2 People ›

Text Message
Monday 4:33 PM

+1 (916) 900-1022

mayor, just following up to
connect you with rick from gov
app. rick, mayor whaley is a
rock star! will let you both take
it from here.

Mayor Whaley,

Pleasure to meet you. Would
love to find a time to tell you
about our public safety
technology and how we are
helping cities become safer
while helping their homeless
community. Do you have any
available time this month to
meet?

Kevin Johnson introducing CHS Derek Bluford to Mayor Whaley

*Mayor Catherine Pugh and Mayor Eric Garcetti - Photo Credit to The Associated Press -
Photographer: Charles Krupa*

*Mayor Catherine Pugh discussing her book, "Healthy Holly" - Photo Credit to Baltimore
Business Journal - Photographer: Melody Simmons*

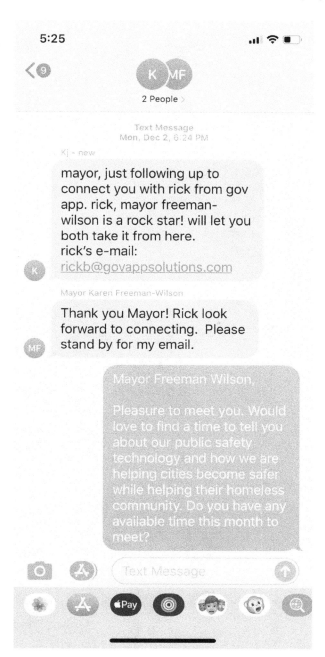

Mayor Johnson introducing FBI CHS Derek Bluford to Mayor Freeman-Wilson

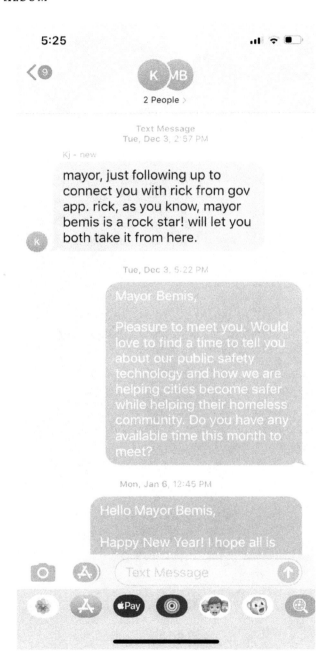

5:25

K **MB**

2 People >

Text Message
Tue, Dec 3, 2:57 PM

Kj - new

mayor, just following up to connect you with rick from gov app. rick, as you know, mayor bemis is a rock star! will let you both take it from here.

Tue, Dec 3, 5:22 PM

Mayor Bemis,

Pleasure to meet you. Would love to find a time to tell you about our public safety technology and how we are helping cities become safer while helping their homeless community. Do you have any available time this month to meet?

Mon, Jan 6, 12:45 PM

Hello Mayor Bemis,

Happy New Year! I hope all is

Text Message

Mayor Johnson introducing The Lobbyist to Mayor Bemis

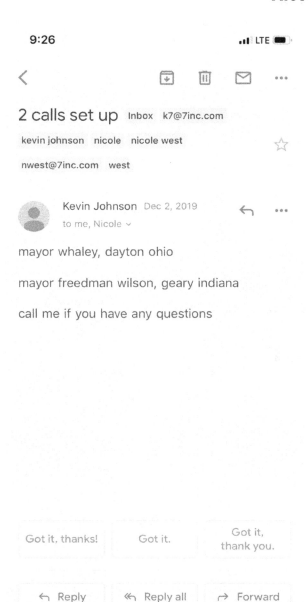

Mayor Johnson setting up more meetings with Mayors

9:26 •••ıl LTE ▬

Kevin Johnson Dec 2, 2019
to me, Nicole ⌄

get it ?

On Dec 2, 2019, at 6:22 PM, Rick B
<dblu87@gmail.com> wrote:

• • •

me Dec 2, 2019
Yep 👍

Kevin Johnson Dec 3, 2019
to me, Nicole ⌄

3 more calls

mayor bemis, gresham oregon

mayor warren, fontana ca

mayor holt, oklahoma city ok

• • •

Mayor Kevin Johnson & +1 530-401-4386

Oct 24, 2017 at 3:46 PM

hey scott, hope you're well. would love for you to set up a next week for sac city folks (u and maria) and rick bluford from text-to-ticket.

text-to-ticket is a great tech tool not just for public safety, but it can also generate revenue for the city ... will let you and rick take it from here.

Thanks, Mayor.

Rick- nice to meet you! Happy to set-up a meeting for next week.

Thanks, Mayor Johnson!

Scott, thanks for the message. We are pretty flexible to meet next week. Would love to get something on the calendar. Thanks in advance

Will do. Just text me your email and I'll get right on it.

Rick@TextToTicket.com
Steve@TextToTicket.com
Paul@TextToTicket.com

Thx! Will be in touch.

Awesome! Thanks again

Dec 7, 2018 at 12:36 PM

Hey, how's it going

Hey Rick.. pretty sure there's a meeting on the books with your team for next Friday . let me know if I'm mistaken.

Mayor Kevin Johnson setting up meeting with City of Sacramento heads after office introducing Derek Bluford

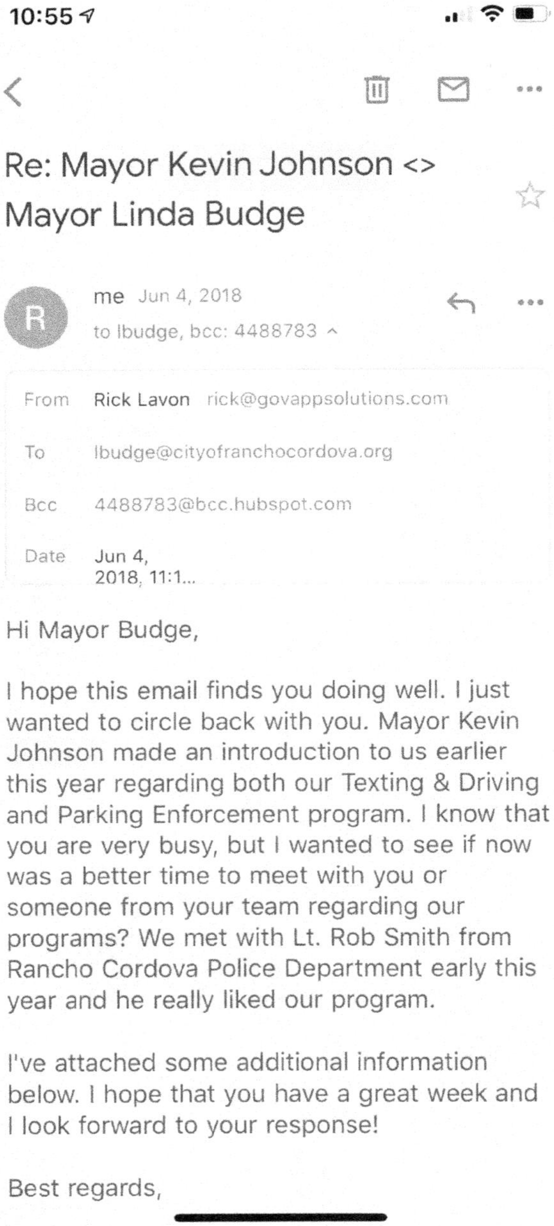

10:55

Re: Mayor Kevin Johnson <>
Mayor Linda Budge

me Jun 4, 2018
to lbudge, bcc: 4488783

From	**Rick Lavon** rick@govappsolutions.com
To	lbudge@cityoffranchocordova.org
Bcc	4488783@bcc.hubspot.com
Date	Jun 4, 2018, 11:1...

Hi Mayor Budge,

I hope this email finds you doing well. I just wanted to circle back with you. Mayor Kevin Johnson made an introduction to us earlier this year regarding both our Texting & Driving and Parking Enforcement program. I know that you are very busy, but I wanted to see if now was a better time to meet with you or someone from your team regarding our programs? We met with Lt. Rob Smith from Rancho Cordova Police Department early this year and he really liked our program.

I've attached some additional information below. I hope that you have a great week and I look forward to your response!

Best regards,

Mayor Linda Budge

1:25 ⏀

.ıl LTE 🔋

‹ 6

+1 (916) 275-9505 ›

Fri, Sep 13, 4:54 PM

mayor svante myrick

My personal cell is
3157508304

he's game to meet

Sweet! And I heard from
Phoenix

game over

Right!?! Should I hit him now or
tomorrow?

yes - now

Mayor Svante Myrick

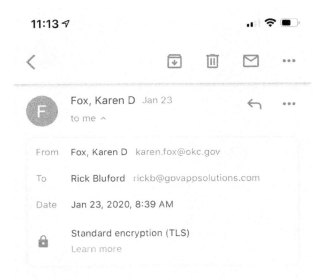

11:13

From   Fox, Karen D   karen.fox@okc.gov

To   Rick Bluford   rickb@govappsolutions.com

Date   Jan 23, 2020, 8:39 AM

Standard encryption (TLS)
Learn more

Good morning ~

Wonderful! I have you scheduled for 2:30pm on March 3rd. I'll contact you again to remind/confirm. The meeting will convene at City Hall which is located at 200 North Walker Avenue and we ask you to check in at Suite 302. For your convenience, there is metered parking around the building or you may utilize one of the parking garages in the area. We can validate the parking charges for the Sheridan & Walker garage (approx. one block South) . Or if you utilize the streetcar system, there is a stop at the Metropolitan Library and the building is across the street from it.

Have a good week.

| Thank you. | Sounds great, thank you! | Confirmed, thank you! |

Oklahoma City Mayor meeting

9:47   .ıl LTE 🔋

<   　　　　　　🗑 🗑 ✉ ...

Tony J Motola Mar 21, 2018   ↩ ...
to me ⌄

Hi Rick-

Same here.

I have passed the application information and the
details of our conversation along to Commander
Sean Connolly in the Police Department.

Commander Connolly is the Department's City
Manager Liaison and can help in routing your
request.

Sean.Connolly@phoenix.gov

Thanks and please keep me posted.

Best,

...

R   me Apr 2, 2018
     Hi Tony, Hope that you had a good weekend. W...

*Phoenix Police Department and Mayors Office email FBI CHS Derek
Bluford*

251

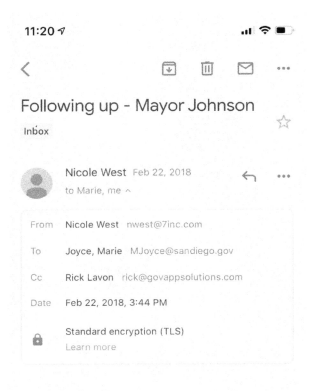

11:20 ⌁

Following up - Mayor Johnson

Inbox ☆

Nicole West Feb 22, 2018 ↩ •••
to Marie, me ∧

From	Nicole West nwest@7inc.com
To	Joyce, Marie MJoyce@sandiego.gov
Cc	Rick Lavon rick@govappsolutions.com
Date	Feb 22, 2018, 3:44 PM
🔒	Standard encryption (TLS) Learn more

Hello Marie,

Hope you're well. Thanks again for your help in connecting Mayor Johnson with Aimee.

Quick update – Mayor Johnson talked to Mayor Faulconer last week, and Aimee this week. Aimee agreed to facilitate a meeting between Mayor Faulconer and Rick Lavon about GovApp as a personal favor to Mayor Johnson sometime next week or the following week.

————

San Diego Mayor Meeting - Personal Favor Confirmation

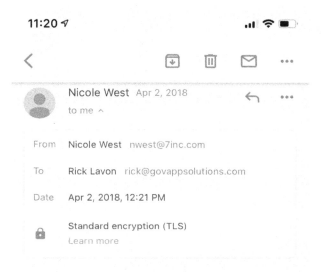

11:20 ✈

Nicole West   Apr 2, 2018

to me ∧

From   Nicole West   nwest@7inc.com

To   Rick Lavon   rick@govappsolutions.com

Date   Apr 2, 2018, 12:21 PM

🔒   Standard encryption (TLS)
     Learn more

Hi Derek,

Hope you had a great Easter!

Your meeting with Mayor Faulconer is confirmed for Wednesday, April 25th from 4:00-4:15 pm in Mayor Faulconer's office at City Hall.

Address:

City of San Diego – City Administration Building

202 C Street, 11th Floor

San Diego, CA 92101

San Diego Mayor Meeting

NEW HAVEN

Andrea Scott-Lindsey (Working Families PAC) - FBI CHS Derek Bluford

Andrea Scott - Envelope

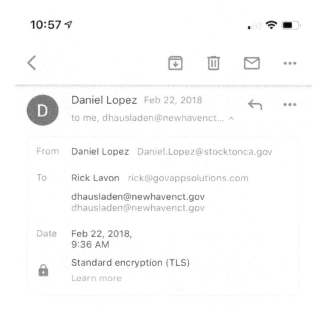

10:57

Daniel Lopez Feb 22, 2018
to me, dhausladen@newhavenct...

From	Daniel Lopez Daniel.Lopez@stocktonca.gov
To	Rick Lavon rick@govappsolutions.com
	dhausladen@newhavenct.gov
	dhausladen@newhavenct.gov
Date	Feb 22, 2018, 9:36 AM
	Standard encryption (TLS)
	Learn more

Thanks Rick, Doug, please let me know how I can be helpful.

Daniel Lopez

Office of Mayor Michael Tubbs

Stockton California

209-292-3516

From: Rick Lavon
[mailto:rick@govappsolutions.com]
Sent: Tuesday, February 20, 2018 9:51 AM
To: Daniel Lopez
<Daniel.Lopez@stocktonca.gov>;
dhausladen@newhavenct.gov
Subject: Daniel Lopez <> Doug Hausladen –

City of Stockton providing fake references for city services to New Haven

255

9:24   .ıl LTE ▮

Sign Up for Procurement website Inbox djones@newhavenct.gov ☆

Daryl Jones Aug 27, 2019
to me ⌄

https://www.newhavenct.gov/
gov/depts/purchasing_division/
general_info/procurement_web_portal.htm

↩ Reply   ↪ Forward

*Darly Jones email FBI CHS Derek Bluford a link to sign up for city
Procurement*

Daryl Jones and FBI CHS Derek Bluford Text

Deposit of the Richard Check into my Derek Bluford checking

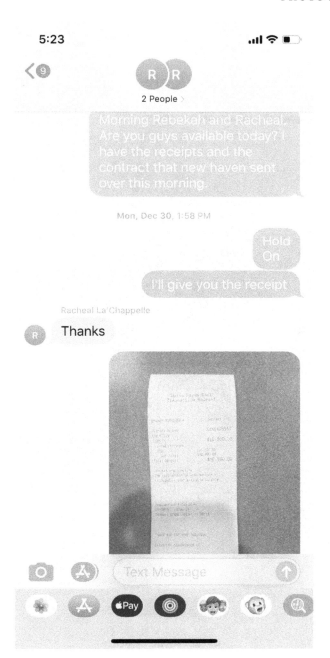

FBI - Derek Bluford confirming deposits of $10,000

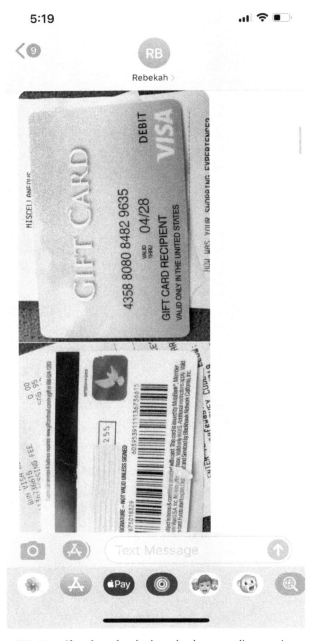

FBI - More gift cards purchased to be used to donate to online campaigns

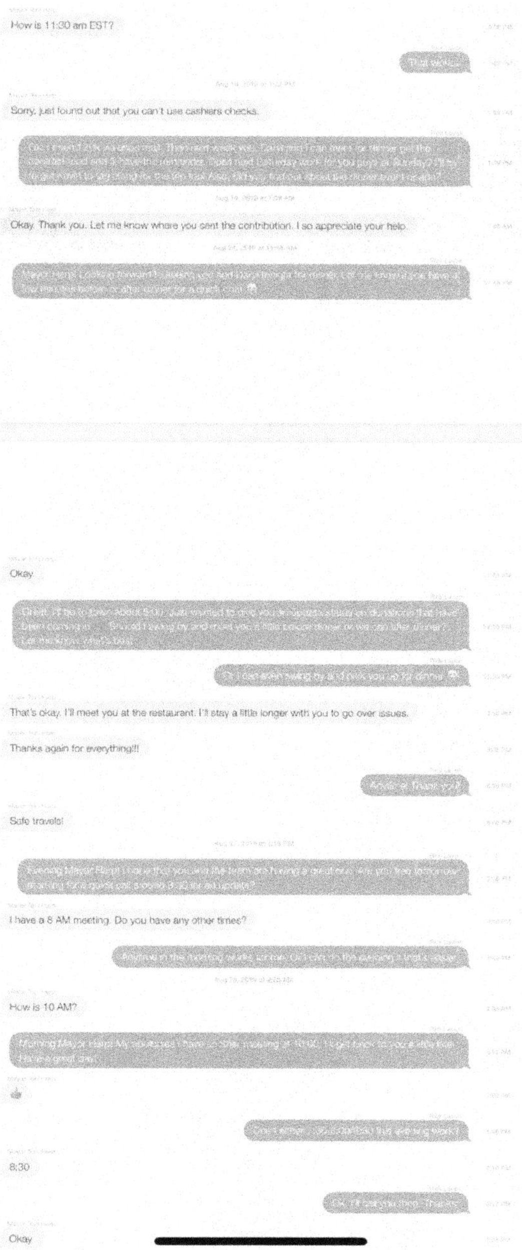

How is 11:30 am EST?

That works.

Sorry, just found out that you can't use cashiers checks.

Okay. Thank you. Let me know where you sent the contribution. I so appreciate your help.

Okay

That's okay. I'll meet you at the restaurant. I'll stay a little longer with you to go over issues.

Thanks again for everything!!!

Safe travels!

I have a 8 AM meeting. Do you have any other times?

How is 10 AM?

I have a 8 AM meeting. Do you have any other times?

8:30

Okay

FBI CHS Derek Bluford _ Mayor Toni Harp text discussing the contract, money and meeting

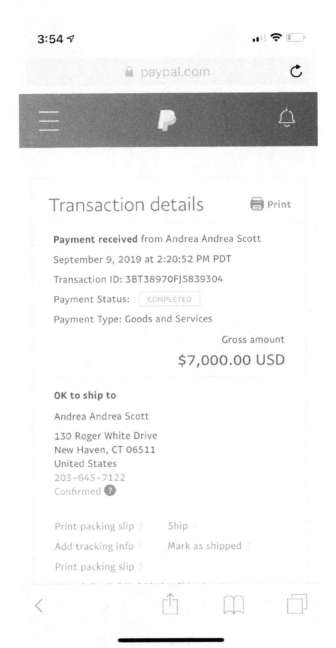

Initial $7,000 sent by Mayor Harps executive Andrea Scott to CHS Derek Bluford - 1 of 2

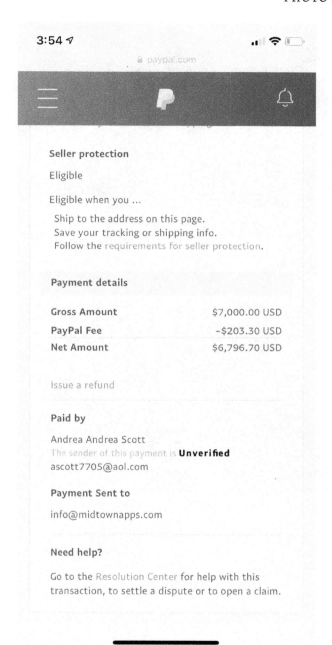

3:54 ⌖   ⏸ 🔋

🔒 paypal.com

Seller protection

Eligible

Eligible when you ...

Ship to the address on this page.
Save your tracking or shipping info.
Follow the requirements for seller protection.

Payment details

Gross Amount	$7,000.00 USD
PayPal Fee	-$203.30 USD
Net Amount	$6,796.70 USD

Issue a refund

Paid by

Andrea Andrea Scott
The sender of this payment is **Unverified**
ascott7705@aol.com

Payment Sent to

info@midtownapps.com

Need help?

Go to the Resolution Center for help with this
transaction, to settle a dispute or to open a claim.

Initial $7,000 sent by Mayor Harps executive Andrea Scott to CHS
Derek Bluford - 2 of 2

Mayor Harp joins Presidential Candidate, Mike Bloomberg - Photo Credit to Hearst Connecticut Media - Photographer: Peter Hvizdak

Mayor Toni Harp and Derek Bluford

Mayor Toni Harp, Andrea Scott, Daryl Jones and FBI CHS Derek
Bluford. Dinner were Mayor Harp took cash from CHS Bluford

Mayor Toni Harp, Mayor Kevin Johnson and others

Mayor Toni Harp - Photo Credit to New Haven Register - Photographer:
Arnold Gold

Messages with Stephanie Mayor Harp Team regarding 30k in payments
coming in

AGREEMENT
BY AND BETWEEN
THE CITY OF NEW HAVEN
AND
GOVERNMENT APP SOLUTIONS, INC.
FOR
PROFESSIONAL SERVICES
REGARDING

A19-1337

PART I

This Agreement, consisting of Parts I and II, Exhibit A and Rider   , entered into this 30th day of December 2019, and effective the 21st day of November, 2019, is by and between the City of New Haven, having an address of 165 Church Street, New Haven, Connecticut 06510 (hereinafter referred to as the 'City'), and Government App Solutions, Inc., with offices at 157 Church Street, 19th Floor, New Haven, CT 06510 (hereinafter referred to as the 'Contractor').

WITNESSETH THAT:

WHEREAS, the City has determined that it requires parking and curbside management services to assist the City with collection of past due amounts arising from parking violations in the City; and

WHEREAS, the City issued, and Contractor responded to RFP Solicitation 2020-08-1306; and

WHEREAS, the City has selected the Contractor and the Contractor has agreed to perform the services for the terms and conditions set forth herein; and

WHEREAS, funds for this Agreement are available from account number 17041010-56694.

NOW, THEREFORE, in consideration of the mutual rights and duties arising out of this Agreement, the City and the Contractor hereby agree as follows:

SECTION 1:   ENGAGEMENT

101. The City hereby engages the Contractor and the Contractor hereby agrees to perform the services set forth herein in accordance with the terms and conditions and for the consideration set forth herein.

102. The person in charge of administering the services described under this Agreement on behalf of the City shall be Daryl Jones, or such other person or persons as may be designated by the City in writing.

New Haven Contract that was issued for bribe Page 1 of 8

267

103. The person responsible for the services to be performed by the Contractor shall be Gagandeep Johal, or such other qualified person as is designated in writing by the Contractor and accepted by the City.

104. The Contractor shall not subcontract any of the professional services to be performed by it under this Agreement, absent written approval by the City. The Contractor shall be as fully responsible to the City for the acts and omissions of its subcontractors, and of persons either directly or indirectly employed by them, as it is for the acts and omissions of persons directly employed by the Contractor.

SECTION 2: SCOPE OF SERVICES

201. The Contractor shall provide to the City services for parking and curbside management in accordance with Exhibit A which is attached hereto and made a part hereof as though fully set forth herein (the "Services"). In the event that any provision of said Exhibit A conflicts with Part I or Part II of this Agreement, Part I or Part II shall be controlling.

The Contractor shall perform the Services set forth under this Agreement in a satisfactory manner, as reasonably determined by the City. The Contractor shall make such revisions or modifications to its work, at its own cost and expense, as may be required by the City, however, the Contractor shall not be required to make revisions at its sole cost and expense where the revisions are based upon considerations outside the scope of Services initially given to the Contractor.

202. Contractor shall cooperate and coordinate data sharing with United Public Safety, Inc., or its successor, responsible for providing certain parking and curbside management services, including issuance of citations. Information sharing is critical for provision of Services.

203. All drawings, reports, and documents prepared by the Contractor under this Agreement, if any, shall be submitted to the City for review. Any such drawings, reports and documents shall be the exclusive property of the City of New Haven. The City will review and, as applicable, respond to materials submitted by the Contractor within a reasonable time frame. In the event the City disapproves of any of the submitted materials, or any portion thereof, or requires additional material in order to properly review the submission, the Contractor shall revise such disapproved work at its own cost and expense and submit the revised work or the additional required material for review and approval.

204. In performing the Services required under this Agreement, the Contractor shall consult with the City and shall meet, as appropriate, with other City employees or officials and with other persons or entities, as necessary, including State and Federal officials and/or neighborhood groups or organizations.

SECTION 3: INFORMATION TO BE FURNISHED TO THE CONTRACTOR

301. The City may provide the Contractor with such documents, data, and other materials in its possession appropriate to the Services to be performed hereunder, and will endeavor to

2

New Haven Contract that was issued for bribe Page 2 of 8

secure materials or information from other sources available to the City, as may be requested by the Contractor, for the purpose of carrying out Services under this Agreement.

302. The Contractor may use the information supplied under Section 301 only in conjunction with the Services to be performed pursuant to this Agreement.

SECTION 4: TIME OF PERFORMANCE AND TERMINATION

401. The Contractor shall perform the Services set forth in Section 2 of this Agreement at such times and in such sequence as may be directed by the City.

402. This Agreement shall remain in effect until the Services required hereunder are completed to the satisfaction of the City, unless otherwise terminated by the parties hereto, but in any event shall terminate on 30 June 2020. The City may renew this Agreement for up to five (5) annual terms, at its option.

403. Termination of Agreement for Cause. If, through any cause not the fault of the City, the Contractor shall fail to fulfill in a timely and proper manner its obligations under this Agreement, or if the Contractor shall violate any of the covenants, agreements, or stipulations of this Agreement, the City shall thereupon have the right to terminate this Agreement by giving written notice to the Contractor of such termination and specifying the effective date thereof, at least five (5) business days before the effective date of such termination. In the event of such termination, all finished or unfinished documents, data, studies, and reports prepared by the Contractor under this Agreement shall, at the option of the City, become its property.

Notwithstanding the above, the Contractor shall not be relieved of liability to the City for damages sustained by the City by virtue of any breach of this Agreement by the Contractor, and the City may withhold any payments to the Contractor for the purpose of setoff until such time as the exact amount of damages due the City from the Contractor is determined.

404. Termination for Convenience of the City. Notwithstanding any other provision in this Agreement, the City reserves the right to terminate this Agreement for its convenience, including for any reason other than for cause, as described in Section 403 above, upon twenty-one (21) days written notice to the Contractor. The Contractor shall be paid for satisfactory Services rendered up to the termination date upon submission to the City of all written memorandums, reports or other partially complete or incomplete documents, and such other materials as will reasonably facilitate transfer to a new Contractor.

SECTION 5: COMPENSATION

501. The City shall compensate the Contractor for satisfactory performance of the Services required under Section 2 of this Agreement, at a rate of eighteen percent (18%) of amounts collected from outstanding citations. Citations are deemed to be outstanding if (i) remain unpaid 365 days from issuance and (ii) are not engaged in an appeal.

3

New Haven Contract that was issued for bribe Page 3 of 8

502. Compensation provided under this Section 5 constitutes full and complete payment for all costs assumed by the Contractor in performing this Agreement including but not limited to: salaries; consultant fees; costs of materials and supplies; printing and reproduction; meetings; consultations; presentations; travel expenses; postage; telephone; clerical expenses; and all similar expenses. No direct costs shall be reimbursed by the City.

503. The City may pay certain out-of-pocket expenses in advance, as follows:

- Court costs
- Up to three mailings per citation at a rate of $0.90 per mailing, plus postage.

Contractor shall invoice the City not less than quarterly nor more frequently than weekly for out-of-pocket expenses. Contractor shall have no obligation to advance court costs or mailing expenses prior to payment of such invoice. The Contractor shall submit invoices electronically via email submission to the City of New Haven's Accounts Payable department at the following email address: NHInvoice@newhavenct.gov.

504. Contractor shall remit amounts recovered to the City, less fees and costs, not less than quarterly. The City may require the Contractor to submit to it such additional information with respect to the Contractor's costs as the City deems necessary. The City may inspect Contractor's books and records relative to the Services, at any time during normal business hours. The City reserves the right to audit Contractor's records relative to the Services at its convenience and expense.

505. No contract for employment is intended or implemented by this Agreement and no fringe benefits will be paid to the Contractor hereunder. The Contractor's relationship to the City is that of an independent contractor.

SECTION 6: INSURANCE AND INDEMNIFICATION

601. Contractor shall defend, indemnify and hold harmless the City of New Haven, and its officers, agents, servants and employees, from and against any and all actions, lawsuits, claims, damages, losses, judgments, liens, costs, expenses and reasonable counsel and consultant fees sustained by any person or entity ("Claims"), to the extent such Claims are caused by the acts, errors or omissions of the Contractor, including its employees, agents or subcontractors, directly or indirectly arising out of, or in any way in connection with, the obligations of the Contractor pursuant to this Agreement.

602. See attached Rider A which provisions, by this reference, are part of this Agreement as if fully incorporated herein.

SECTION 7: TERMS AND CONDITIONS

701. This Agreement is subject to and incorporates the provisions attached hereto as City of New Haven Contract for Professional or Technical Services Part II, Terms and Conditions. In

4

New Haven Contract that was issued for bribe Page 4 of 8

the event any provision of said Part II conflicts with any provision of this Part I of this Agreement, Part I shall be controlling.

702. This Agreement, its terms and conditions and any claims arising therefrom, shall be governed by Connecticut law. The Contractor shall comply with all applicable laws, rules, ordinances, regulations and codes of the State of Connecticut and the City of New Haven. In addition, the Contractor shall comply with all applicable Federal laws, codes, rules and regulations.

703. The parties agree that they waive a trial by jury as to any and all claims, causes of action or disputes arising out of this Agreement or Services to be provided pursuant to this Agreement. Notwithstanding any such claim, dispute, or legal action, the Contractor shall continue to perform Services under this Agreement in a timely manner, unless otherwise directed by the City.

704. The City and the Contractor each binds itself, its partners, successors, assigns and legal representatives to the other party to this Agreement and to the partners, successors, assigns and legal representatives of such other party with respect to all covenants of this Agreement.

705. This Agreement incorporates all of the understandings of the parties hereto as to the matters contained herein and supersedes any and all agreements reached by the parties prior to the execution of this Agreement, whether oral or written, as to such matters. Unless specifically revised in Exhibit A, this Agreement incorporates by this reference the obligations, agreements and representations of the Contractor as required by the City's Request For Proposal #2020-08-1306, and any addendum thereto, (the "City's RFP") and as submitted in, or acknowledged by submission of, the Contractor's response to the City's RFP and any addendum thereto.

706. If any provision of this Agreement is held invalid, the balance of the provisions of this Agreement shall not be affected thereby if the balance of the provisions of this Agreement would then continue to conform to the requirements of applicable laws.

707. Any waiver of the terms and conditions of this Agreement by either of the parties hereto shall not be construed to be a waiver of any other term or condition of this Agreement.

708. The City may, from time to time, request changes in the scope of Services of the Contractor to be performed hereunder. Such changes, including any increase or decrease in the amount of the Contractor s compensation, which are mutually agreed upon by and between the City and the Contractor, shall be incorporated in written amendments executed by both parties to this Agreement.

709. References herein in the masculine gender shall also be construed to apply to the feminine gender, and the singular to the plural, and vice versa.

5

New Haven Contract that was issued for bribe Page 5 of 8

710. Article headings are for the convenience of the parties only and do not describe or limit the contents of the Section.

711. Failure of the Contractor to comply with any provision of this Agreement is a Contractor default under this Agreement and the City reserves any and all rights including self-help, termination pursuant to Section 403 herein and any and all other remedies available to the City at law or in equity.

712. Except as otherwise specifically provided in this Agreement, whenever under this Agreement notices, approvals, authorizations, determinations, satisfactions or waivers are required or permitted, such items shall be effective and valid only when given in writing signed by a duly authorized officer of the City or the Contractor, whichever is applicable, and delivered in hand or sent by mail, postage prepaid, to the party to whom it is directed, which until changed by written notice, are as follows:

Contractor: Gagandeep Johal, CEO
                 Government App Solutions
                 157 Church Street
                 New Haven, CT 06510

City: Daryl Jones, Controller
                 City of New Haven
                 200 Orange Street, Third Floor
                 New Haven, CT 06510

New Haven Contract that was issued for bribe Page 6 of 8

IN WITNESS WHEREOF, the parties have executed two (2) counterparts of this Agreement No. A19-1337 as of the day and year first above written.

WITNESSES:

CITY:
CITY OF NEW HAVEN

By: _Toni N. Harp_
Toni N. Harp
Mayor

Approved as to Form and Correctness:

Catherine E. LaMarr
Deputy Corporation Counsel

WITNESSES:

Meredith Merth

Meredith Merth

CONTRACTOR:
GOVERNMENT APP SOLUTIONS, INC.

By: _____
Name: Gagandeep Johal
Its: 12/30/19
Duly Authorized

7

New Haven Contract that was issued for bribe Page 7 of 8

<u>CITY OF NEW HAVEN</u>
<u>CONTRACT FOR PROFESSIONAL OR TECHNICAL SERVICES</u>
<u>PART II - TERMS AND CONDITIONS</u>

1.   <u>Personnel</u>. (a) The Contractor represents that it has, or will secure at its own expense, all personnel required in performing the services under this Agreement. Such personnel shall not be employees of or have any contractual relationship with the City.

(b)   All the services required hereunder will be performed by the Contractor or under its supervision and all personnel engaged in the work shall be fully qualified and shall be authorized or permitted under State or local law to perform such services.

(c)   No person who is serving a sentence in a penal or correctional institution shall be employed on work under this Agreement. The foregoing sentence shall not be interpreted to interfere with the Contractor's compliance with the City's Ban the Box requirements.

2.   <u>Anti-Kickback Rules</u>. Salaries of architects, draftsmen, technical engineers, and technicians performing work under this Agreement shall be paid unconditionally and not less often than once a month without deductions or rebate on any account except only such payroll deductions as are mandatory by law or permitted by the applicable regulations issued by the Secretary of Labor pursuant to the "Anti-Kickback Act" of June 13, 1934, as now codified in 18 U.S.C. $ 874 and 40 U.S.C. $ 3145. The Contractor shall comply with applicable "Anti-Kickback" regulations and shall insert appropriate provisions in all subcontracts covering work under this Agreement to ensure compliance by subcontractors with such regulations, and shall be responsible for the submission of affidavits required of subcontractors thereunder except as the Secretary of Labor may specifically provide for variations or exemptions from the requirements thereof.

3.   <u>Withholding of Salaries</u>. If, in the performance of this Agreement, there is any underpayment of salaries by the Contractor or by any subcontractor thereunder, the City shall withhold from the Contractor out of payments due to him an amount sufficient to pay to employees underpaid the difference between the salaries required hereby to be paid and the salary actually paid such employees for the total number of hours worked. The amounts withheld shall be disbursed by the City for and on account of the Contractor or subcontractor to the respective employees to whom they are due.

4.   <u>Claims and Disputes Pertaining to Salary Rates</u>. Claims and disputes pertaining to salary rates or to classifications of architects, draftsmen, technical engineers, and technicians performing work under this Agreement shall be promptly reported in writing by the Contractor to the City, and the City's decision regarding such claims and disputes shall be final. Particularly with respect to this Section and Section 5 above, the City reserves the right to inspect Contractor's records with respect to this Agreement and specifically, without limiting the generality of the foregoing, payroll and employee records with respect to the work performed pursuant to this Agreement.

New Haven Contract that was issued for bribe Page 8 of 8

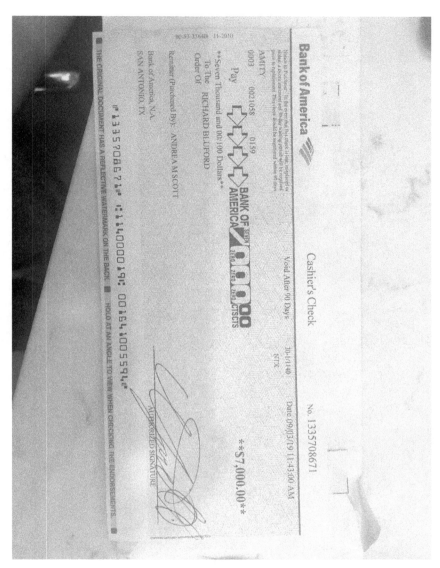

Over payment to Returned to Richard Bluford by Mayor Toni Harps Aid Andrea Scott -
Check

Working families Receipt

The business check mailed to Working Family Pac

PHOENIX

CHS Derek Bluford setting up meeting with Phoenix Mayor Kate Gallego

1:25 ⏎   .␣ LTE ▮

‹ 6

+1 (916) 275-9505 ›

Thu, Sep 26, 11:33 AM

KJ TO ITHACA MAYOR

hello mayor ,

following up : rick is going to
call you today and tomorrow ...
pls try to pick up or return his
call ...

thank you sir

Sun, Sep 29, 2:23 PM

Hey Kev,

Talked to Phoenix. Mayor is
trying to meet us both. Any
days good for you in October?
I'll cover your flight 🙈

Sun, Sep 29, 5:12 PM

10.2, 10.3

*CHS Derek Bluford and Mayor Johnson discussing travel to Phoenix to
meet with new Mayor Kate Gallego*

Congressman Greg Stanton - Fake Robbery News Story - Photo Credit to ABC -
Photographer: ABC15 Arizona (taken from video)

Greg Stanton, official portrait, 116th Congress - Photo Credit to United
States Congress - Photographer: United States Congress

11:00

Automatic reply: Intro: Mayor
Kevin Johnson to Mayor Greg
Stanton - Texting & Driving
Program Inbox

Mayor Stanton MYR Feb 7, 2018
to me

From	Mayor Stanton MYR Mayor.Stanton@phoenix.gov
To	Rick Bluford rick@govappsolutions.com
Date	Feb 7, 2018, 3:02 PM
🔒	Standard encryption (TLS) Learn more

Thank you for contacting us. Please be aware that
the email message you sent is: (1) subject to
disclosure under the Public Records Law, (2) not
private or confidential and (3) retained for 90 days.
An email sent on this system is a public record and
may be viewed immediately by the media and/or
public and could become part of a future public
records request. Please DO NOT reply to this
message. This message is for information only.

↩ Reply   ↪ Forward

FBI CHS Derek Bluford emails Greg Stanton

280

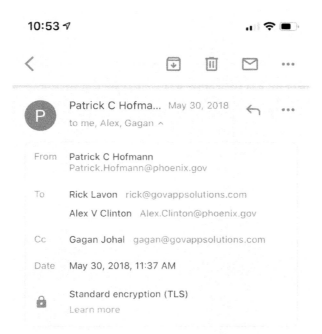

Thank you, I will be reviewing the attached information and will forward to my chain of command for review.

Patrick C. Hofmann, Lieutenant
Phoenix PD Traffic Bureau
302 E. Union Hills Drive
Phoenix, AZ 85024
Desk: (602)-495-6701
Cell:(602)-531-4150
patrick.hofmann@phoenix.gov

PRIDE
Protection | Respect | Integrity |Dedication | Excellence

NOTICE: This communication contains information that is law enforcement sensitive for official use only, sensitive but unclassified, proprietary, privileged, and may be legally protected or otherwise exempt from disclosure. You are hereby notified that any disclosure, dissemination, copying or distributing of this transmission is strictly prohibited.

From: Rick Lavon <rick@govappsolutions.com>

Lt. Patrick Hoffman - Phoenix Police Department

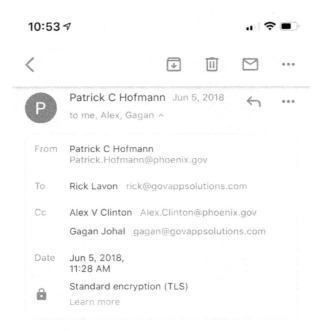

10:53

From   Patrick C Hofmann
           Patrick.Hofmann@phoenix.gov

To   Rick Lavon rick@govappsolutions.com

Cc   Alex V Clinton Alex.Clinton@phoenix.gov

         Gagan Johal gagan@govappsolutions.com

Date   Jun 5, 2018,
         11:28 AM

🔒   Standard encryption (TLS)
     Learn more

Hello Rick,

I am still waiting for directives from my chain of command before I move forward with any approvals. I sent them a reminder this morning and should hear back from them soon.

I will reach out to you when I have more information.

Thank you,

Patrick C. Hofmann, Lieutenant
Phoenix PD Traffic Bureau
302 E. Union Hills Drive
Phoenix, AZ 85024
Desk: (602)-495-6701
Cell:(602)-531-4150
patrick.hofmann@phoenix.gov

PRIDE
Protection | Respect | Integrity |Dedication | Excellence

NOTICE: This communication contains information that is law enforcement sensitive for official use only, sensitive but unclassified proprietary privileged and may be

Lt. Patrick Hoffman confirming awaiting direction from Chief

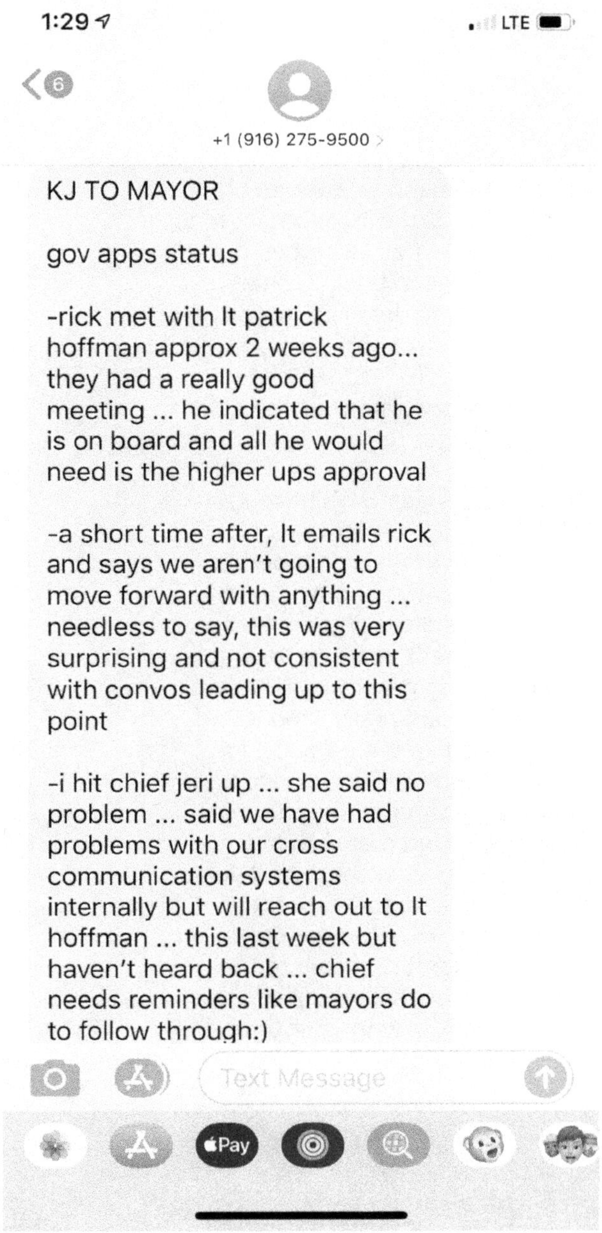
1:29
LTE
6
+1 (916) 275-9500
KJ TO MAYOR

gov apps status

-rick met with lt patrick hoffman approx 2 weeks ago... they had a really good meeting ... he indicated that he is on board and all he would need is the higher ups approval

-a short time after, lt emails rick and says we aren't going to move forward with anything ... needless to say, this was very surprising and not consistent with convos leading up to this point

-i hit chief jeri up ... she said no problem ... said we have had problems with our cross communication systems internally but will reach out to lt hoffman ... this last week but haven't heard back ... chief needs reminders like mayors do to follow through:)
Text Message
Pay

Mayor Johnson - Mayor Stanton discussing pushing a contract through the city and contacting the Chief of Police to get it done - 1 of 3

+1 (916) 275-9500 >

communication systems internally but will reach out to lt hoffman ... this last week but haven't heard back ... chief needs reminders like mayors do to follow through:)

-fyi here's what i sent the chief a week ago :

hope all is going well. wanted to reach out regarding a company that i introduced to mayor stanton and his team. they have a parking enforcement app and texting and driving program. the mayor and his team really liked it and thought it would be good for the city so he reach out to lt. patrick hofmann. the team went out and met with him about two weeks ago and your officers liked it. i know they offered to give the parking enforcement program to the city for free. any chance you can check in with your team

Mayor Johnson - Mayor Stanton discussing pushing a contract through the city and contacting the Chief of Police to get it done - 2 of 3

1:29 ✈

.ıll LTE 🔋

‹ 6

+1 (916) 275-9500 ›

went out and met with him about two weeks ago and your officers liked it. i know they offered to give the parking enforcement program to the city for free. any chance you can check in with your team and see where things are?

-bottom line mayor: can u inquire ... getting us across the finish line would be huge ... if there is a legit reason to not move forward than so be it

thanks mayor

MAYOR
Will make some calls.

KJ
can't thank u enough

this could be a game changer if we can get this done ...
promise

Jun 15, 2018, 9:00 AM

Mayor Johnson - Mayor Stanton discussing pushing a contract through the city and contacting the Chief of Police to get it done - 2 of 3

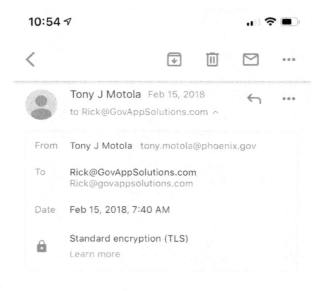

10:54

From   Tony J Motola   tony.motola@phoenix.gov

To   Rick@GovAppSolutions.com
       Rick@govappsolutions.com

Date   Feb 15, 2018, 7:40 AM

🔒   Standard encryption (TLS)
       Learn more

Hi Rick,

The Mayor asked that I speak with you on this issue.

I would be glad to schedule a phone call. See how you are Monday 2/26 between 1-2pm MST – I think you are an hour behind us right now. Or Wed 2/28 between 2-3pm MST.

If those don't work we will find some that do. My direct line is 602-534-1275.

Thanks

_____

Mayor Stanton directing staff to connect with me regarding contract

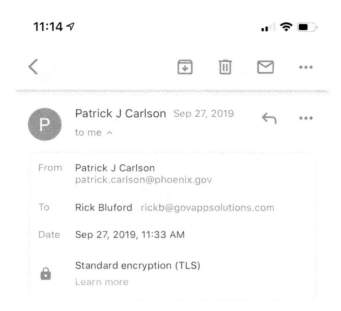

11:14

Patrick J Carlson Sep 27, 2019

to me ^

From   Patrick J Carlson
        patrick.carlson@phoenix.gov

To   Rick Bluford   rickb@govappsolutions.com

Date   Sep 27, 2019, 11:33 AM

🔒   Standard encryption (TLS)
        Learn more

Hey Rick,

Hope all is well. Looking at the calendar, when will you and Fmr. Mayor Johnson be in Phoenix next? Mayor's calendar is busy at the end of next week but I'll try to make it work when you're available.

Phoenix Meeting

PHOTO ALBUM

Tony from Mayor Stantons team confirming Lt. Patrick Hoffman will take it from there

PRESIDENTIAL ELECTION

Elizabeth Warren Page 1 of 10

Derek Bluford - Brooklyn - Page 2 of 10

PHOTO ALBUM

 Gmail

Rick Bluford <dblu87@gmail.com>

JetBlue booking confirmation for DEREK BLUFORD - QOWTIC
1 message

JetBlue Reservations <jetblueairways@email.jetblue.com>
Reply-To: JetBlue Reservations <reply@email.jetblue.com>
To: dblu87@gmail.com

Sun, Jan 5, 2020 at 10:39 AM

Check out the details for your trip on Sun, Jan 05

Please note: This is not your boarding pass.

Your confirmation code is

QOWTIC

Change made easy.

Switch or cancel flights, add extras like
Even More Space or pets, update your
seat assignment, TrueBlue & KTN
numbers, and other traveler details—all in
one place.

You can also manage your trips by
downloading our free mobile app.

Flights

Date   Sun, Jan 05

https://mail.google.com/mail/u/1?ik=55bfa96dd8&view=pt&search=all&permthid=thread-f%3A1654914651020972042&simpl=msg-f%3A18549146510 ...   1/6

Elizabeth Warren Page 3 of 10

Gmail - JetBlue booking confirmation for DEREK BLUFORD - QOWTIC

SFO

San Francisco, CA

Terminal: 1 North

JFK

New York, NY

Departs	11:59pm
Arrives	8:23am
Flight	1516

jetBlue

JFK

New York, NY

Terminal: 5

SFO

San Francisco, CA

Date	Sun, Jan 12
Departs	3:30pm
Arrives	7:24pm
Flight	915

jetBlue

If your booking was made at least 7 days in advance, you may cancel it within 24 hours without a cancellation fee. Please click here for details on our change and cancel policies.

Traveler Details

DEREK BLUFORD

Frequent Flier: B6 3286996150

Ticket number: 2792142115426

SFO - JFK:

Fare: Mint

Bags: Two (2) checked bags, one (1) carry-on, one (1) personal item.*

Seat: 3F

Notes: Even More Speed

JFK - SFO:

Fare: Blue

Bags: One (1) carry-on, one (1) personal item. This fare

Elizabeth Warren Page 4 of 10

8/10/2020

option does not include checked bags.

Seat: 23E

EVEN MORE

Get up to 7" more legroom, a fast lane to the TSA checkpoint*, and early boarding—all the better to nab that overhead bin.

Add Even More Space ▶

*Select cities

Payment Details

Visa
XXXXXXXXXXX1741

NON REFUNDABLE		$1,586.97
Taxes & fees		$147.82
Total:		**$1,734.79**
		USD

Purchase Date: Jan 5, 2020

Request full receipt

AVIS
Budget

The wheel deal.

Save with Avis and Budget when you add a car to your booking, plus drive away with TrueBlue points on every rental.

Add a car ▶

Flight Tracker   Bag Info   Airport Info

https://mail.google.com/mail/u/1?ik=55bfa96dd8&view=pt&search=all&permthid=thread-f%3A1654914651020972042&simpl=msg-f%3A16549148510...   3/6

Elizabeth Warren Page 5 of 10

Stay Connected

 Download the JetBlue
mobile app

✈ Flights   Hotels

✈ Flights + Hotel   🚗 Cars
     by JetBlue Vacations

Help

Business Travel

Privacy

About JetBlue

CUSTOMER CONCERNS

Any customer inquiries or concerns can be addressed here, emailed to dearjetblue@jetblue.com, or sent to JetBlue Airways, 6322 South 3000 East, Suite G10, Salt Lake City, UT 84121.

NOTICE OF INCORPORATED TERMS

All travel on JetBlue is subject to JetBlue's Contract of Carriage, the full terms of which are incorporated herein by reference, including but not restricted to: (i) Limits on JetBlue's liability for personal injury or death, and for loss, damage, or delay of goods and baggage, including special rules for fragile and perishable goods; (ii) Claims restrictions, including time periods within which you must file a claim or bring an action against JetBlue; (iii) Rights of JetBlue to change the terms of the Contract of Carriage; (iv) Rules on reservations, check-in, and refusal to carry; (v) JetBlue's rights and limits on its liability for delay or failure to perform service, including schedule changes, substitution of aircraft or alternate air carriers, and rerouting; (iv) Non-refundability of reservations. International travel may also be subject to JetBlue's International Passenger Rules Tariffs on file with the U.S. Department of Transportation and, where applicable, the Montreal Convention or the Warsaw Convention and its amendments and special contracts. The full text of the Contract of Carriage is available for inspection at book.jetblue.com and all airport customer service counters. Tariffs may also be inspected at all airport customer service counters. You have the right to receive a copy of the Contract of Carriage and tariffs by mail upon request.

NOTICE OF INCREASED GOVERNMENT TAX OR FEE

JetBlue reserves the right to collect additional payment after a fare has been paid in full and tickets issued for any additional government taxes or fees assessed or imposed.

CARRY-ON BAGGAGE RULES

In general, customers are restricted to: one (1) carry-on item that must be placed in the overhead bin and must not exceed external dimensions of 22in. x 14in. x 9in; and one (1) small personal item, such as a purse, briefcase, laptop computer case, small backpack, or a small camera, which must fit completely under the seat in front of the customer. Please visit book.jetblue.com for additional information and exceptions. On any given flight, JetBlue reserves the right to further restrict the number of carry-on items as circumstances may require.

CHECKED BAGGAGE ALLOWANCE/FEES

For Blue / Blue Basic / Blue Extra fares, the first checked bag fee is $30 and the second checked bag fee is $40. For Blue Plus fares, one checked bag is included and the second checked bag fee is $40.

Elizabeth Warren Page 6 of 10

For Mint fares, two checked bags are included. For TrueBlue Mosaic members: two checked bags are included. For JetBlue Plus cardmembers, one checked bag is included and the second checked bag fee is $40. You can add up to 2 checked bags in advance (more than 24 hours before departure) and save $1 on each bag fee. For all fares, the fee for the third (or more) checked bag is $150 and only available at the airport. All bags are subject to size/weight restrictions. Other fees apply for oversized or overweight baggage. See www.jetblue.com/bags. Excess baggage rules and size/weight restrictions may vary depending on load availability and country restrictions. See www.jetblue.com/bags for more information. Travel on our partner airlines (excluding Cape Air*) --- Baggage rules and fees vary by partner airline and destination. JetBlue will follow our partner airlines' fees when customers are traveling on an itinerary including one of our partner airlines. See http://www.jetblue.com/partners for more information.

*For itineraries with a connection only to/from Cape Air. JetBlue's standard fees apply.

CHECK-IN TIMES

For domestic travel, customers traveling with checked baggage must obtain a boarding pass and check their baggage no less than forty (40) minutes prior to scheduled departure and be onboard the aircraft no less than fifteen (15) minutes prior to the scheduled or posted departure time. Customers traveling without checked baggage must obtain a boarding pass no less than thirty (30) minutes prior to scheduled departure and be onboard the aircraft no less than fifteen (15) minutes prior to scheduled or posted departure time. For international travel, all customers must obtain a boarding pass and check their baggage no less than sixty (60) minutes prior to scheduled departure and be onboard the aircraft no less than fifteen (15) minutes prior to the scheduled or posted departure time.

DOCUMENTATION REQUIREMENTS

For domestic travel, customers over the age of 18 must present government-issued photo identification that includes a tamper resistant feature, name, date of birth, gender, and expiration date. Documents required for international travel vary according to country of travel, citizenship, residency, age, length of stay, purpose of visit, etc., and customers should contact the embassy or consulate in their destination country for all documentation requirements, including proof of return or onward travel. It is your responsibility to ensure you have the required documentation for travel. JetBlue reserves the right to deny boarding to anyone without proper documentation and is not responsible for any failure by you to have the required documentation for entry into a foreign country or return into the United States.

ADVICE TO DOMESTIC CUSTOMERS ON CARRIER LIABILITY

For travel entirely within the U.S., JetBlue's liability for loss, damage or delay in delivery of baggage is limited to $3,500 per ticketed passenger unless a higher value is declared in advance and additional charges are paid. JetBlue assumes no responsibility for fragile, unsuitably packaged, irreplaceable, essential, or perishable items. Please refer to JetBlue's Contract of Carriage for additional information.

ADVICE TO INTERNATIONAL PASSENGERS ON LIMITATION OF LIABILITY

Passengers on a journey involving an ultimate destination or a stop in a country other than the country of departure are advised that international treaties known as the Montreal Convention, or its predecessor, the Warsaw Convention, including its amendments, may apply to the entire journey, including any portion thereof within a country. For such passengers, the treaty, including special contracts of carriage embodied in applicable tariffs, governs and may limit the liability of JetBlue in respect of death or injury to passengers, and for destruction or loss of, or damage to, baggage, and for delay of passengers and baggage. If your journey also involves carriage by other airlines, you should contact them for information on their limits of liability. Please refer to JetBlue's Contract of Carriage for additional information, including the limits of liability for services provided in the European Union.

NOTICE OF OVERBOOKING OF FLIGHTS

While JetBlue does not intentionally overbook its flights, there is still a slight chance that a seat will not be available on a flight for which a person has a confirmed reservation. If the flight is overbooked, no one will be denied a seat until airline personnel first ask for volunteers willing to give up their reservation in exchange for a payment of the airline's choosing. If there are not enough volunteers, JetBlue will deny boarding to other persons in accordance with its particular boarding priority. With few exceptions, including failure to comply with JetBlue's check-in deadlines, persons denied boarding involuntarily are entitled to compensation. Please refer to JetBlue's Contract of Carriage for the complete rules for the payment of compensation and JetBlue's boarding priorities. Some airlines do

Elizabeth Warren Page 7 of 10

Gmail - JetBlue booking confirmation for DEREK BLUFORD - QOWTIC

not apply these consumer protections to travel from some foreign countries, although other consumer protections may be available. Check with your airline or your travel agent.

© 2020 JetBlue Airways

Elizabeth Warren Page 8 of 10

Gmail

Rick Bluford <dblu87@gmail.com>

Your receipt from Airbnb
1 message

Airbnb <express@airbnb.com>   Sun, Jan 5, 2020 at 8:29 AM
To: dblu87@gmail.com

 airbnb

Your receipt from Airbnb

Receipt ID: RCY9BE8HZ3 · Jan 05, 2020

New York

6 nights in New York

Mon, Jan 06, 2020 — Sun, Jan 12, 2020
Entire home/apt · 2 beds · 1 guest
Confirmation code: HMTBMHWKZY
Go to listing

Price breakdown

Reservation change: Price adjusted

Price difference	$81.57
Total adjustment (USD)	**$81.57**

Elizabeth Warren Page 9 of 10

or (iv) Airbnb's Guest Refund Policy Terms, available at airbnb.com/terms... Questions or complaints: contact Airbnb Payments, Inc. at 888-4-AIRBNB (888-424-77821).

Elizabeth Warren Page 10 of 10

ROCHESTER

Mayor Kevin Johnson - Mayor Lovely Warren - CHS Derek Bluford

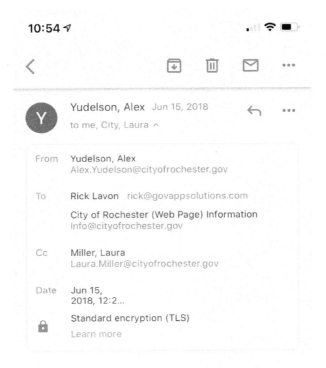

10:54

Yudelson, Alex Jun 15, 2018

to me, City, Laura

From	Yudelson, Alex Alex.Yudelson@cityofrochester.gov
To	Rick Lavon rick@govappsolutions.com
	City of Rochester (Web Page) Information info@cityofrochester.gov
Cc	Miller, Laura Laura.Miller@cityofrochester.gov
Date	Jun 15, 2018, 12:2...
🔒	Standard encryption (TLS) Learn more

Rick,

Sorry for the delay in response. I am adding
Laura Miller, our Parking Director, to the email
chain here. If she sees an opportunity to utilize
your program, she can reach out to have a
conversation about it.

All the best,

Alex Yudelson

• • •

Mayor Lovely Warren directs staff to reach out to me to start contract
process. Rochester New York

SACRAMENTO

City of Sacramento - RAILS Grant Passed

City of Sacramento - RAILS Meeting

Coworking Business that Kevin Johnson & Derek Bluford owned with others

Darrell Steinberg and Kevin Johnson -Photo Credit to California Senate Democrats -
Photographer: California Senate Democrats (image taken from video)

Derek Bluford - Sacramento BizX Conference

Derek Bluford and Mayor Kevin Johnson at City Hall - Gift Acceptance

Derek Bluford at St.Hope event - Barry Bonds

Derek Bluford at St.Hope event

Derek Bluford win Sacramento Kings Owner winning NBA Startup Competition - Photo
Credit to Comstock Magazine - Photographer: John Jacobs

Mayor Kevin Johnson & Commissioner Donald Stern - Photo Credit to
Kevin Johnson (@KJ_MayorJohnson) - Photographer: Kevin Johnson

Mayor Kevin Johnson - City Of Sacramento Meeting - Photo Credit to GBM News
(webpage active from 2007 to 2016) - Photographer: Stephen Crowley

Mayor Kevin Johnson - Photo Credit by Gina Yanez - Photo Credit to
Eleakis & Elder Photography - Photographer: Eleakis & Elder Photography

SAN FRANCISCO

Derek Bluford - San Francisco City Hall

STATE CAPITOL

Assemblymen Jim Cooper, Mayor Kevin Johnson, Michelle Rhee, Derek Bluford and others

Derek Bluford at Capital for meeting

Derek Bluford entering State Capitol

Mayor Johnson texting FBI CHS Derek Bluford to Connect him with Assemblyman Jim Cooper

Mayor Kevin Johnson - Jim Cooper - CHS Derek Bluford

STOCKTON

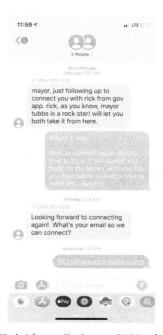

Mayor Kevin Johnson - Jim Cooper - CHS Derek Bluford

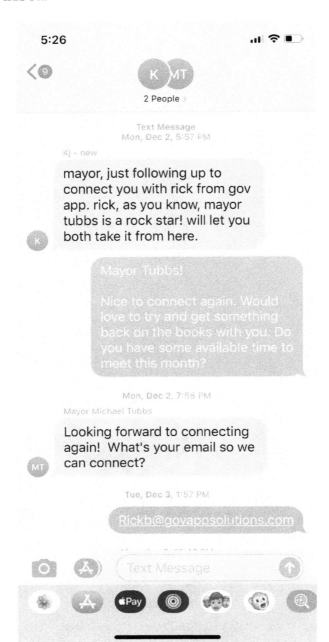

Mayor Johnson, Mayor Tubbs and FBI CHS Derek Bluford

Mayor Michael Tubbs and Daniel Lopez - Photo Credit to The Sacramento Bee - Photographer Hector Amezcua

Mayor Michael Tubbs and Derek Bluford

Mayor Michael Tubbs and Presidential Candidate Mike Bloomberg - Photo Credit to The New York Times - Photographer Salgu Wissmath

Mayor Michael Tubbs and Senator Kamala Harris - Photo Credit to The United States Senate - Office of Senator Kamala Harris Photographer: The United States Senate - Office of Senator Kamala Harris

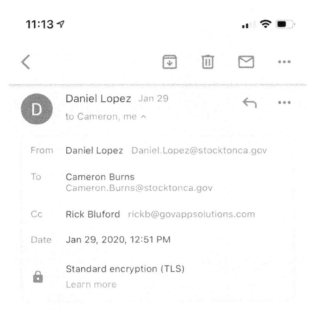

11:13 ⏀

Daniel Lopez Jan 29
to Cameron, me ⌄

From   Daniel Lopez Daniel.Lopez@stocktonca.gov

To   Cameron Burns
        Cameron.Burns@stocktonca.gov

Cc   Rick Bluford rickb@govappsolutions.com

Date   Jan 29, 2020, 12:51 PM

🔒   Standard encryption (TLS)
        Learn more

Cameron,

Rick Bluford and former Mayor Kevin Johnson are looking to meet with Mayor Tubbs here in Stockton. Are there times this Friday or early next week that would work?

Thanks,

Daniel Lopez

Office of Mayor Michael Tubbs

Stockton California

209-292-3516

Stockton - Mayor Johnson and Mayor Tubbs meeting

VENTURE CAPITAL

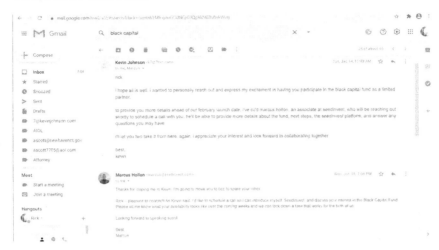

Kevin Johnson, CHS Bluford, and SeedInvest 1 of 2

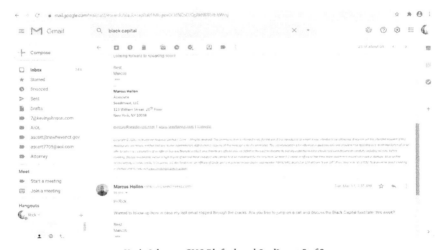

Kevin Johnson, CHS Bluford, and SeedInvest 2 of 2

SeedInvest CEO Ryan Feit, Mayor Kevin Johnson, and other - Photo Credit to SeedInvest -
Photographer: SeedInvest

Troy Carter and Mayor Kevin Johnson

Troy Carter and Mayor Kevin Johnson

NOTES

CHAPTER 2

1. Stanford Law School, Stanford University, "The Law Firm of the Future," March 4, 2015, https://law.stanford.edu/event/the-law-firm-of-the-future/.
2. Jennifer Pike, "Quicklegal's Winning Experience at Techweek's Launch," Metova, December 5, 2014, https://metova.com/quicklegals-winning-experience-at-techweeks-launch/.
3. Raheem F. Hosseini and Steph Rodriguez, "The Problem with K.J.'s Comeback," *Sacramento News & Review,* November 14, 2019, https://www.newsreview.com/sacramento/problem-with-k-j-s-comeback/content?oid=29248405.
4. Ben van der Meer, "Petrovich, Court Ruling Upholds What I've Said All Along," *Sacramento Business Journal,* April 9, 2020, https://www.bizjournals.com/sacramento/news/2020/04/09/petrovich-court-ruling-upholds-what-ive-said-all.html.
5. Kevin Johnson, address to US Conference of Mayors, June 30, 2014.
6. Vito, "Accused Sexual Abuser Kevin Johnson Meets with Accused Sexual Abuser Donald Trump," *Buzz,* 2016, https://www.topvirallists.com/accused-sexual-abuser-kevin-johnson-meets-with-accused-sexual-abuser-donald-trump/.
7. Matt Bonesteel, "Three of Kevin Johnson's Accusers Speak to HBO's 'Real Sports' about Alleged Molestation," *The Washington Post,* March 23, 2016, https://www.washingtonpost.com/news/early-lead/wp/2016/03/23/three-of-kevin-johnsons-accusers-speak-to-hbos-real-sports-about-alleged-molestation/.

CHAPTER 4

1. Ben Shapiro, *The People vs. Barack Obama: The Criminal Case against the Obama Administration,* Threshold Editions, 2014, 190.
2. Joe Kinsey, "Who the F@CK Is That Guy!" *Busted Coverage,* November 6, 2008, https://bustedcoverage.com/2008/11/06/who-the-fck-is-that-guy-kevin-johnson-wins-sacramento-mayor-election-grows-facial-hair-now-white/.

CHAPTER 5

1. Lindsey McPherson, "Arizona Congressional Candidate Greg Stanton Was Victim of Armed Robbery," *Roll Call,* October 15, 2018, https://www.rollcall.com/2018/10/15/arizona-congressional-candidate-greg-stanton-was-victim-of-armed-robbery/.

CHAPTER 6

1. Howie Kussoy, "Teen Who Accused Ex-NBA Star Kevin Johnson of Sexual Abuse Tells Her Story," *New York Post*, September 25, 2015, https://nypost.com/2015/09/25/ex-nba-star-groomed-me-for-teen-fondling-alleged-victim/.

CHAPTER 7

1. Jeremy B. White, "California Ponders Whether Prostitutes Are Criminals or Victims, *Sacramento Bee*, February 28, 2016, https://amp.sacbee.com/news/politics-government/capitol-alert/article62833612.html.

CHAPTER 9

1. "L.A. Clippers Owner to GF: Don't Bring Black People to My Games . . . Including Magic Johnson," *TMZ Sports*, April 25, 2014, https://www.tmz.com/2014/04/26/donald-sterling-clippers-owner-black-people-racist-audio-magic-johnson/.
2. Ryan Lillis, "Sterling Controversy Catapults Sacramento Mayor Kevin Johnson onto National Stage," *Sacramento Bee*, April 29, 2014, https://www.sacbee.com/news/local/news-columns-blogs/city-beat/article2597443.html.
3. David Zahniser, John Rubin, Emily Alpert Reyes, and Andrea Castillo, "FBI Raids Home and Offices of L.A. City Councilman Jose Huizar," *Los Angeles Times*, November 7, 2018, https://www.latimes.com/local/lanow/la-me-ln-jose-huizar-investigation-20181107-story.html.

CHAPTER 10

1. "Public Corruption," *FBI*, https://www.fbi.gov/investigate/public-corruption.

CHAPTER 11

1. Dave McKenna, "Secret Emails Show Kevin Johnson Spying On, Attempting to Bankrupt Enemies," Deadspin, July 26, 2016, https://deadspin.com/secret-emails-show-kevin-johnson-spying-on-attempting-1784042899.

CHAPTER 12

1. Alexis McCombs, "Kevin Johnson Builds St. Hope to Help Our Kids: K-12 Charter Schools Turn Neighborhood Around," *Black Enterprise*, https://www.questia.com/magazine/1G1-156135657/kevin-johnson-builds-st-hope-to-help-our-kids-k-12.

2. Byron York, "UPDATE: AmeriCorps Scandal Figure Un-Invited from AmeriCorps Conference," *Washington Examiner,* June 10, 2010, https://www. washingtonexaminer.com/update-americorps-scandal-figure-un-invited-from-americorps-conference.
3. Byron York, "AmeriCorps Scandal Figure Invited to AmeriCorps Conference," *Washington Examiner,* June 9, 2010, https://www.washingtonexaminer.com/americorps-scandal-figure-invited-to-americorps-conference.

CHAPTER 13

1. Ryan Lillis, "Sterling Controversy Catapults Sacramento Mayor Kevin Johnson onto National Stage," *Sacramento Bee,* April 29, 2014, https://www.sacbee.com/news/local/news-columns-blogs/city-beat/article2597443.html
2. "President Obama Remarks to US Conference of Mayors," C-SPAN, January 23, 2015, https://www.c-span.org/video/?323967-2/president-obama-remarks-us-conference-mayors.

CHAPTER 14

1. Cassie Da Costa, "How the FBI Brought Down One of the Youngest Mayors Ever," Daily Beast, April 24, 2020, https://www.thedailybeast.com/how-the-fbi-brought-down-jasiel-correia-the-youngest-mayor-ever.
2. "Fall River Mayor Charged with Extorting Marijuana Vendors for Cash," US Department of Justice US Attorney's Office District of Massachusetts, September 6, 2019, https://www.justice.gov/usao-ma/pr/fall-river-mayor-charged-extorting-marijuana-vendors-cash.

CHAPTER 21

1. Nate Cohn, "Did Comey Cost Clinton the Election? Why We'll Never Know," *The New York Times,* June 14, 2018, https://www.nytimes.com/2018/06/14/upshot/did-comey-cost-clinton-the-election-why-well-never-know.html.

CHAPTER 22

1. John Gramlich, "Only 2% of Federal Criminal Defendants Go to Trial, and Most Who Do Are Found Guilty," Pew Research Center, June 11, 2019, https://www.pewresearch.org/fact-tank/2019/06/11/only-2-of-federal-criminal-defendants-go-to-trial-and-most-who-do-are-found-guilty/.

CHAPTER 23

1. "Fifth Amendment—US Constitution," *FindLaw,* https://constitution.findlaw.com/amendment5.html/